Predict Through Numerology

Predict Through Numerology

S. JAFAR MAHMUD

BOOKS FOR ALL
DELHI - 110052

Sales Office
D.K. Publishers Distributers (P) Ltd.
1, Ansari Road, Darya Ganj
New Delhi - 110002
Phones : 3261465, 3278368
Fax : 091-011-3264368

First Published 1997

Published by :
BOOKS FOR ALL
B-2, Vardhman Palace,
Nimri Commercial Centre,
Ashok Vihar, Phase-IV,
Delhi - 110 052
Tel. : 7401672

Printed at :
D. K. Fine Art Press (P) Ltd.
Delhi - 110 052

PRINTED IN INDIA

Contents

Interpreting the Numbers

1. **Number 1** stands for the Sun, and all that is strong, individual, and creative, Number 1 people are both leaders; they are ambitious and active, and often dominant and aggressive. This is a powerful number, and it augurs success. It is the number of innovators, Leaders winners-but also of tyrants! Number 1 people can be very self- entered, ruthless, and stubborn if crossed, and their chosen career or activity will probably receive more energy and associated with their personal relationships. Sunday is the day associated with the sun with the number 1.

2. **Number 2** The Moon, and Monday are associated with the number 2. Number 2 people are more gentle, passive and artistic that the stronger number 1 characters. Number 2s are more geared to thought that to action, and although they are inventive, they will be less forceful in carrying out their plans. They are likely to have charm and powers of intuition, but they likely to have charm and powers of intuition, but they may suffer form a lack of self-confidence. Number 2 people can be changeable-perhaps even deceitful - and may be over-sensitive and may be over-sensitive and depressive. Number 2 people get on well with their opposites, the number 1 people.

3. **Number 3** Energetic disciplined, talented, number 3 people often achieve success in their chosen fields. In fact, they are seldom satisfied with less, as they conscientious, very proud and independent, and they love to be in control. They may be too fond of telling other people what to do, but they have many qualities. A superficial show may hide considerable spirituality, since 3s the number of the Trinity. Number 3 people have good relationships with others 3s, and those born under6 and 9. Jupiter is the planet of this number, and Thursday is the luckiest day for number 3 people.

4. **Number 4** - number of seasons, the elements, the points of the compass - is oriented to the earth, and its people may be steady and practical, with great endurance. Yet number 4 - the square - contains its own opposite, and number 4 people often see everything form the opposite point of view, making them rebellious and unconventional. They are seldom interested in material things. Making friends is hard is for 4s, are they may feel isolated. People whose numbers are 1,2,7 and 8 are the best friends or partners for 4s. Number 4s associated with the planet Uranus, and with Sunday.

5. **Number 5** - the number of the senses - symbolizes the planet Mercurial in all their characteristics. Lively, sensual, pleasure-seeking, impulsive, quick- tempered, these highly -strung number 5 people may have trouble with nerves. They are good at making money, especially by risk or speculation, and they bounce back easily from any failure. They make friends easily with people born under any other number, but close friends will probably be fellow number 5s. Wednesday

is the luckiest day for the quicksilver number 5.

6. **Number 6** A " perfect" number because it is the sum of its factors (1,2,3), 6 is balanced harmonious, and is associated with family love and domesticity. Number 6 people are very reliable and trustworthy, but they may also be obstinate. Their planet, Venus, governs devotion in love, but number 6 people are romantic rather than sensual. They have a great love of beauty; they are usually attractive and have a greater ability to make friends than any other number. Despite a hatred of any sort of discord, they can be obstinate fighters. Their luckiest day is Friday.

7. **Number 7** is thought to have occult significance, and people born under its influences often have a strongly philosophical or spiritual outlook - they are not usually interested in material things. They may be highly intuitive, even psychic. Number 7 People often exert a mysterious influence over others, but may also have a tendency to become too introverted. They are original thinkers, and have the luck associated with their number. Their planet is Neptune, which is associated with water, and number 7 people often have a restless love of travel and of the sea. Monday is their luckiest day.

8. **Number 8** is a strange, difficult number. It is twice 4, and so incorporates the rebellious contradictions of that number. Number 8 may mean sorrow, yet it is also associated with worldly success. Number 8 people have great willpower and individuality, but they may appear cold. In fact they have deep and intense feelings, and are often misunderstood by others. Their planet is Saturn, and Saturday is their most important day.

9. **Number 9** is sometimes considered the ultimate number, with special or even sacred significance. When multiplied by any number, it reproduces itself (eg3*9=27, 2+7=9). Number 9 symbolizes the planet Mars, and its people fighters - active and determined, they usually succeed after a struggle, but they are prone to accident and injury, and may be quarrelsome. But at its best number 9 will influence the highest qualities of courage and brotherly love. Number 9 people should try to carry out their plans on Tuesday, the day governed by their planet. Mars.

Importance of Birth Numbers

The birth number is the easiest and clearest to use everyday matters and for all those who are not advanced students in occult symbolism. It is indicates with authority and decision the exact date for action, namely, a date which will be in accord and harmony with the birth number and the rules concerning it are simple and easy to understand.

A person, born on say 1, 10, 15, 28th of any month will be called the feminine or negative side of the 1, he or she can take this number as an associate number, but on account of the peculiar qualities of this number 1 I do not advise it to be chosen for any worldly or material affairs. This number 4 will generally be found 1 persons as coming into their lives 'on its own,' if I may be permitted to describe its action as such, but more in the nature of a fatalistic number which has an influence on their lives outside of their control and certainly not always connected with the happier side of life. In many instances of number 1 people in my collection, the number 4, such as the 4th, 13th, 22nd, and 31st, has brought on these dates the news of an accident, a death, or a sorrow which has played some important part in their lives. The number 1 people also often find that they seem unconsciously to be drawn to live houses whose number makes a 4, such as a house in a terrace or street numbered 4, 13, 22, 31, 40, 49, etc., and although such houses may be proved to be associated with important events in the career, yet I have seldom found them associated with happy material advantages.

A Person whose Birth number is an 8 should certainly never live in a house whose number makes a 4, 13, 22, 31, 40, etc., and neither should a person whose Birth number makes a 4 live in a house whose number makes a 8, 17, 26, 35, 44, etc., not at least if they wish to escape sorrow, misfortune, and strange fatelity.

The second best numbers for a person whose Birth number makes a 1are interchangeable number of the 2-7, and dates these number make, such as the 2nd, 7th, 11th 16th, 20th, 25th, or 29th, and houses under the numbers 2, 7, 11, 16, 20, 25, 29, 34, etc., are generally not unfavourable; but as these number are related to change or unsettled conditions, the number 1 person seldom settles down in houses under the 2-7 numbers, or finds conditions brought into his for life under the dates given by these numbers as relating to fixed or settled matters.

Under the law of harmony and vibration, there is no question but that number 1 persons should be associated as much as possible with the same number 2 in all its forms. Persons born under the 3 should employ their number 3, and so on for all the number with the exception of those born under the 4 and the 8. In the latter cases I recommend, then not to increase the peculiar influence of the 4 and 8, but to choose more fortunate vibrations.

This is where the power and knowledge of the Name number will apply. A number 4 or a number 8 person who desires to get under more fortunate vibrations, as they cannot alter their Birth number they can at least change their Name number and live under it and so become equally as fortunate as those whose Birth number is a lucky one.

I will give an example of what I mean.

Suppose a man or woman has been born on, say, the 8th, 17th or 26th of January, and the Name number works out, let us say, to a final total of a 1, 3, 5, or 6 (I have purposely taken the strong or positive numbers). Then I most certainly advise the number 8 persons to drop using the 8 in all their transactions and use instead any strong number the name may give, such as a 1, 3, 5, or 6, and a number 4 person should do lidewise.

You will notice I have not used the 9 in giving this rule, and my reason for not doing so is that the 4, which is the symbol of the planet Uranus , and the 8, which represents the Planet Saturn, are so antagonistic in their qualities to the 9, the symbol of Mars of Mars, that it is better to keep such numbers apart.

This may sound strange to those who have not made any study of occultism, but believe me, the above rule is not laid down at random or by any shadowy guess-work; on the contrary, it has a solid foundation in the science of the planets, and anyone who has ever studied Astrology will tell you that I am right when I say that any combination of the planets of Mars (9) and Saturn (8) or Uranus (4) can only foreshadow troubles and disasters of all kinds.

To resume, reason I advise that the Birth number is the most important as the Key to the main 'fadic' number influencing the life in the first place it is unalterable; secondly, it is related to the planet's influence at the moment of birth, and thirdly, by some mysterious law of vibration - which, even if we do not understand , we must admit to exist even in such so - called inanimate objects as crystals, molecules, and atoms - the moment of birth decides the note of harmony or vibration, and so has its influence on the actions of our lives from the cradle to the grave.

Further, the birth number relates to the material side of life, the name number to the more occult or spiritual side of our existence.

Also the name number is more difficult to be sure of - it must be the product of the name we are most known by. This presents a problem for the average man or woman. Many men are more known by their surnames than by their Christian and surname together, and many women are called by some 'pet' name to the complete extinction of their Christian name. In working out such cases mistakes may easily be made and a number allotted which is not the true one, whereas by going by the birth number and using it as the foundation no mistake can be made.

If, then, it is found that the name one thinks is the correct one and if its number gives the same number or any degree of the same number as the birth number, then one can be absolutely certain that no mistake is being made, for if both the name number and the birth number accord there is nothing one can desire better.

If the name number does not accord with the birth number, it can be made to agree by the addition of an initial or an alteration in the Christian name, so that both give the same vibration; and I advise this to be done all in every case where the birth and name number do not agree, except in the case of the numbers 4 and 8 which I have spoken of ealier in this chapter.

Those who are advanced students in occult symbolism can utilise the hidden meaning given by both Christian and surnames to work out the finer shades of destiny, but for all ordinary cases - and I must not lose sight of the fact that I am writing this book for the average man and woman, those who want to help themselves in the easiest possible way, and who have, perhaps, no time for deep and abstruse study-to all those, I know I cannot do better than to advise them to follow closely the rules governing the birth number as set out in these pages.

Note: The number on the month of birth or the year of birth is not so personal or so intimate in regard to close calculations as in the number of the day of birth.

The number of the month is useful as far as general matters, and the number of the year to the wider current of events.

Example: A person born , say, on the 6th June, 1866 write this down in the following order:

6th	=	6(Individual or personal)
June	=	5(General Matters)
1866 = 21	=	3(Current of Destiny)

The numbers 6, 5 and 3 should be regarded as separate and distinxt and not added together.

The year number totaled and added to itself indicates an important year in the Destiny.

Example 1866 = 21

21

1887

A further illustration of this is given later in the case of will I am I of Prussia.

As it is impossible in a book of this size to go into every shade of the occult significance of numbers that spring from foundation of 1 to 9, must confine myself to giving a few foundation of 1 to 9, I must confine myself to giving a few illustrate of how to use the number allotted to the letters of the Hebrew alphabet for the purpose of showing how Destiny appears interwoven with number and names-

The great Napoleon originally wrote his name as Napoleon Buonaparte. Later on in his life he changed it to Napoleon Bonapate. This change had a curious signfficance:

Napoleon equals in numbers a 5

Bounapate equals in numbers a 5.

The number 5, as I showed earlier in these pages, is considered a magical number and was carried by the ancient Greeks as Mascot when they went into battle. The two numbers of 5, if added, producing 10, are equally important and streangely significant in this case.

When Napoleon altered the spelling to Bonapate, it altered the vibration of this world to an 8, and if refer to what I said about this number you will find on the lower plane if represents revolution, anarchy, waywardens, conflict with human justice, and on the lower plane a tragic ending to the life. Although a great man, Napoleon was on the lower plane of existence, as can be seen if one looks up how the number 8 (Saturn) and the 9 (Mars) dominated the chief events of his career. As Napoleon Bonaparte the two names total the number 13, which number, in the occult symbolism which accompanies this system of letters and numbers, bears the curious picture of a skeleton with a scythe mowing men down, also a symbol of 'power' which 'if wrongly used will bring destruction upon itself'.

This was no borne out by Napoleon's career that further comment is unnecessary.

Some remarkable illustration of the significance of names and numbers may be had from examples of ships.

The United States battleship Maine, which so mysteriously exploded in Havana Harbour, and in which every man on board was lost, gives for the word 'Maine' the number 16 for its compounded number, the symbolism for this number being, as you will have read earlier, 'A Tower Struck by Lighting.' The mystery of the blowing up of this warship has never been solved, but it caused the declaration of war by the United States against Spain.

Another tragic ship disaster was that of the waratah which, after leaving Australia, sank with all her passengers and crew as if she had been swallowed up by the ocean. The number of the word 'Waratah' equals 20, which, as you have read in Chapter 63, is called 'the Judgement'. This number is symbolised by the figure of a winged angel sounding a trumpet, while from below a man, a woman, and a child are seen rising from a tomb with their hands clasped in Prayer.

Yet another illustration might be taken from the fate of the Lienster, the Holyhead and Kingstwon mail-boat that was torpedoed by a German submarine within sight of the Irish coast during the last months of the 1914-1918 War.

The word 'Leinster' gives the compound number of 28, a number full of contradictions.' Which also indicates 'loss through trust in others'. This boat was carrying a large number of soldiers as well as passengers, who certainly trusted their lives to others, in the belief that the boat would be accompanied by some of the destroyers from Kingstown Harbour. For some unexplained reason the order to the destroyers never-come - the Leinster sailed alone, and in less than an hour met fate and the loss of several hundred lives.

I know two men who at the last moment avoided going on that boat on that particular night by noticing that the compound numbers of their names made 28, the same number as the Leinster, and as they had read that in this system of symbolism it is not a fortunate number, and being struck by the coincidence of the name of the boat making the same number, both men took their luggage off at last moment, and so escaped.

It is quite natural that under the tension of war people are more inclined to watch for the slightest clue that might give a warning of danger. I known of many instance where men actually saved their lives by following the clue given by this system of numbers. In one case a man resting by the side of his battery was amusing asking the birth dates of the men around him. He was startled to find that they were all born under number 8, he himself born on the 26th January, a number 8 man in the 'period of the 8.'It had just dawned on him that the day of the month also happened to be an 8, namely the 17th February, and looking up, he counted the number of the battery: it was also an 8. Just than a german gun opened fire. He counted the shells as they dropped, each one coming nearer and nearer. As the seventh fell he could not resist the dread that overcame him - rushed out into the open, and as he did so, the eight shell strcuk his battery-he was the only one who escaped.

Among my collection on the influence of number in connection with events, I have many that are decidedly interesting.

The following appeared in many of the London newspapers:

Sir Alma-Tadema, the famous artist, says his important number is 17. He was 17 when he first wife; their first house had that number: it was on August 17th that the work of rebuilding his home began, and on November 17th that he took up his residence there. His second marriage was in 1871, -and here 17 is the result of the figures added together. His house, in the artistic quarter of St. John's Wood, was again a multiple of 17. Alma-Tadema was born on January 8th, which would account for the 17th, which given the single number 8, having such importance in his life.

King Edward VI was born on the 9th November in a month that is called in Astrology 'second house of Mars' and governed by 9, the number of Mars.

His marriage took place in the year 1863, which numbers added to the other make 9; he was to have been crowned on the 27th of June, which figures togther make 9, and he was actually crowned on August 8th.

King Edward often referred to me as the man who would not let him live past 69'. On the occasion when I first had the honour of meeting him as Prince of Wales in Lady Arthur Paget's house, he asked me to work out his numbers. I did so and explained the reason his 'fadic' or 'root' bumbers were the 6 and 9, I then told him that when these two numbers came together would be fatal year, and further that the than the event should take place on a his fatal year, and further than the event should take place on a day making the number 6 in a month governed by the 6, which would be may. He never forgot my prediction, and it is my melancholy privilege to record that the last occasion when I had any conversation with his late Majesty was a few weeks before his death. He was joining the royal train at Victoria to make his usual journey to the Continent when he noticed me, I happening also to be going abrod. He sent an equerry to call me, and he said, smiling broadly:

'Well, "Cheiro, "I'm still alive, as you see, but from that warning of yours, as I am now in my 69th year, I must take care' - a reference to the fact that according to the fadic system of numbers his 69th year was for him a dangerous year. He then spoke briefly of his racing wagers, and concluded by emphasising how remarkably me advice had been crowned by success.

Alas, in a view short weeks he returned to Buckingham Place, and the public heard with consternation of his illness, which proved fatal. On May 6th - in his 69th year, the first time that these 'fadic' number came together - my prediction was fulfilled.

Incidentally, King Edward mentioned that his 'dear friend,' as he called him, Lord Randolph Churchill, was extremely superstifious in regard to the number 1, and attributed many adverse events to the fact that born on the 13th of February, 1849, the total of whose numbers 22 also made a 4.

I explained to king Edward that the idea that 13 was an unfortunate number was not supported by occultisim; that it was in fact an important number if persons were born on the 4th, 13th , 22nd or 31st, and it was simply garded as ill-omendd because in occultism it was looked upon with venetration.

A few years before his death in London in January, 1895, I had a brief interview with this famous statesman, and he reminded me that my theory of numbers had interested him very much. From King Edward he had gathered that I thought that 4 was his fadic number, and I confirmed this. It was also represented with almost all the leading events of his life.

Another remarkable instance of prediction by numbers

was in the case of my meeting with the then Sir Charles Russell. I explained to him that his important numbers were the 1 and the 4, with what are called their interchangeable number of 2 and 7, and that the would reach the highest position his career could give him on a date that made a 1, such as the 1st, 10th , 19th or 28th in a month governed by the 2 and 7, such as July, which is goverend by those numbers, and in a year whose number added upto the number of 4. He made a careful note of this, and when he wrote his no bes of Lord Chief M Justice of England for the first time he sent to me to the Law Courts. After the ceremoby of installation was over he come to me in his private room and as a souvenir gave me a signed impression of his hand.

The Significance of Numbers

The ancient Hindu searchers after Nature's laws, if must be remembered, were in former years masters of all such studies but in transmitting their knowledge to their descendants, they so endeavoured to hide their secrets form the common people that in most cases the key to the problem became lost, and the turth that had been discovered become buried in the dust of superstition and charlatanism, to be re-formed, let us hope , when some similar cycle of thought in its own appointed time will again claim attention to this side of nature.

This ancient people, together with the Chaldeans and Egyptians, were the absolute masters of the occult of hidden meaning of numbers, in their application to time and in their relation to human life.

When examining such questions, we must not forget that it was the Hindus who discovered what is known as the precession of the Equinoxes, and their calulation such an occurrence takes place every 25, 827 years; our modern science after labours of hundreds of years has simply proved them to be correct.

How, or by what means they were able to arrive at such a calculation, has never been discovered - observations lasting over such a period of time are hardly admissible, and calculation without instruments is also scarcely conceivable, and so science has only been able, first to accept their statement, and later to asknowledge its accuracy.

Their judgement, together with that of the Chalderns, as to the lenght of that is known as the cycle of years of the planets, has been handed down to us form the most remote ages, and also by our modern appliances has been proved correst, so when one comes to a study such as this, as to the value or the numbers 1 to 9, which, as the seven harmonies of music are the basses of all music that has ever been conceived, these above-stated numbers are the basis of all our numbers and calculations, it is then only logical to accept the decision of those great students of long past ages and at least examine their deductions with a mide free form bias and prejudic.

It is impossible here to give in detail all the reasonings and examples that exist for a belief in the occult side of numbers, but it may interest my readers if I give a few illustrations of why the number 7 has for ages been regarded as the number of mystery relating to the spiritual side of things, and why the number 9 has in it turn come to be regarded as the finality or end of the series on which our materialistic calculations are built but the most casual observer can only admit that beyond the number 9 all ordinary numbers become but a mere repetition of the first 9. A simple illustration of this will readily suffice. The number 10, as the zero is not a number, becomes a repetition of the number 1. The number 11 added together as the ancient occultists laid down in their law of natural addition, namely, adding together from left to right, repeats the number 2, 12, repeats 3, 13 repeats 4, and so on up to 19, which in its turn becomes 1 plus 9 equals 10, and so again the repetition of 1. 20 represents 2, and so on to infinity. The occult symbolism of what are called compound numbers, that is, those numbers from 10 onwards, I will explain later.

In this way it will be seen that in all our materialistic systems of numbers, the numbers 1 to 9 are the base on which we are compelled to build, just as in the same way the seven great or primary harmonies in music are the bases of all music, and again as the seven primary colours are the bases of all our combinations of colours. In passing it may be remarked that all through the Bible and other sacred books, the 'seven,' whenever mentioned, always stands in relation to the spiritual or mysterious God force, and has curious significance in this sense whenever employed.

For a few instances of this, take the seven days (or cycles) of the creation as referred to in Genesis:

The seven heavens, so often referred to.

The seven thrones.

The seven seals.

The seven churches.

The seven days' march round the walls of jericho, when, on the seventh day, the walls fell, before that mysterious, God force symbolised in the number of seven. It is also remarkable that there are exactly seven generations from david to the birth of Christ. In Revelation we read of the 'seven spirits of God sent forth into all the earth. Ezekiel speaks of 'the seven angels of the Lord that go to and for through the whole earth,' which is believed to be a reference to the magnetic influences of the seven creative planets which radiate through the earth.

Again, we have the seven spirits referred to in the Egyptian religion.

The seven Divas of the Hindus 'Bible:

The seven Amschaspands of persaon faith

The seven Angels of the Chaldeans.

The seven Sephiroth of the Hebrew Cabala.

The seven Archangels of Revelation, etc., etc.

Let us now take another view of this strange number. If we were to examine every class of occult teaching from the Hindu, chines, Egyptian, Greek, Hebrew, or modern school, whichever one may choose, in every case- and without a single exception-we shall find that the quality of the number 7 stands for the expression of that mysterious God force in Nature before referred to.

In the most ancient rules of occult philosophy we find the rule laid down that the number 7 is the only number capable of divding 'the number of Eternity,' and continuing in itself as long as the number representing Eternity lasts, and yet, at every addition of itself producing the number 9, or in other words it produces the Basic numbers on which all meterialistic calculations are built, and on which all human beings depend and the whole edifice of human thought finds expression.

Example

The number 1 is the first number. It represents the First Cause, Creator, God, or Spirit, call it, as you like. As circle of the zero 'o', has always been taken as the symbol of endlessness- otherwise Eternity, place the 1 and the figure zero by its side, and you get the significant symbol of eternity such as 1 plus o, the 10 and then places as many of these emblems of eternity side by side as you like, and you get such a figure as 1,000,000. Divide by the mystic number 7 and you get the number 142857.

7) 1,000,000

142857

Add as many zeros as you like, and keep on dividing by the 7, and you yourself may go on through all eternity and you can only get repetitions of the same 142857, which from time immemorial has been called the 'sacred number.' Now add this number wherever you find it by natural addition, it will give you the figure 27. And as you have seen by the rule of natural addition described on a preceding page, you keep adding till only one number,' you add again 27 by natural addition, and 2 plus 7 equals 9, or in other words, you get the full range of the first series of numbers on which all materialisitc or human calculations can be built.

Now, let us return to the symbolism of seven for a

moment. You know, of course, that Buddha is always represented as sitting in center of a Lotus, Let us examine, then, the secret of a Lotus. Let us examine, then secret of such a selection. Is not perhaps generally known that the 7 is reproduced in many strange ways in Nature herself , and that flowers that have been crossed by intermingling with other flowers have their outside petals in the number of seven, but as flowers are so easily crossed with other varieties, and it is so difficult to fine a pure type, Buddha took the Lotus, which never becomes crossed or losses its indivduality, the emblem of the religion he taught, because, first, it seven foundation petals are always in evidence, and further, the religion he taught was that the creative Spirit was the foundation and origin of all things, and thus again bore silent but unmistakable testimony to the creative action of the seven planets which all religions have had their origin,

Long before man made his creeds, or civilisations their laws , the influence of these seven planets had become known on the earth. Out of the dark night of antiquity their light become law and as far we cen penetrate, even to the very confines of prehistori 6days, in all races, in all countries, we find the influence of the seven planets through all and in all.

Days of The Week

The seven days of the week have been the outcome of the influence of the seven creative planets and gave the names of the days of the week, in every land or clime. Take any nation you may choose, this fact remains the same, and is so expressed in almost every language, Chines Assyrian, Hindu, Egypthian, Hebrew, Greek, Latin, French, German, or English. In modern languages Monday or Monday in English becomes Montag in German or Lundi (Lune) in French, Lunes in Spanish, and so on until one comes to Saturday or Saturday, the day on which God ordered the Hebrews that no work should be done, and giving them this command He said, it is a sign between me and the children of Israel for ever. And Saturday, year by year, in our modern civilisation is becoming more and more a day of rest.

In connection with thought, it is worthy of remark that Saturn, the last planet in the series of the seven creative planets of our solar system, in all religions, Hebrew or otherwise, represents 'cessation', or rest from labour in another sense. In this strange example one can see the connection between the seven days of the week and the seven creative planets, and it throws a new light on the verse, 'God made the sun, moon, and stars and appointed, them for signs and for seasons and for days and for years. Even Mr. Maunder, the eminent author of so many works on astronomy, calls attention to this strange division of the week into seven days when he says in his Astronomy of the Bible: 'the period of seven days does not fit precisely into either months or seasons of the year. It is not a division of time that man would man naturally adopt, it runs across all natural division of time, 'but this author, not seeing or perhaps knowing the great hidden truth contained in the number 7, worried only over the point, that it was not a division of time which man would naturally adopt. But as everything on the earth and above the earth has its meaning, and especially its secret or soul meaning, its place, position, and number, in the 'order of things,' which is the highest form of design, every day of the week every hour of the day, and every minute of the hour, has both its meaning and number.

It is invariably conceded by every class of scientist that the regularity, order, and system of the wonderful machinery of the heavens is beyond all comparison.

We known today that the heavenly bodies move through their orbits with such precision that in millions of years they do not vary one minute of time. We know that they exercise an influence on this earth which is felt by the veriest atōms in the earth, though what this force is, or with what incredible speed it acts, my forever remain a mystery. It was in dealing with this mysterious law that the ancient philosophers by study, experiments, concentration of mind, and perhaps intuition, arrived at the fixation of certain laws governing, life, which may be as accurate as their discovery that the ' precession of the Equinoxes takes place once in every 25, 827 years.

It is from these wonderful students of nature that we have received the first idea as to the division of the zodiac into twelve periods of 30 degrees, and further, that each period produces a definite and well-known influence on the earth and on human beings born in any of its twelve periods. They further subdivided these 30-degrees periods into division of three periods of 10 degrees each, in which the planets are also found to have an influence, and they pursued their investigations until they worked out a system demonstrating that each day has its own particular meanings sue to vibrations in the either, which keeps the earth in instantaneous report with its entire solar system, and lastly, that as the sun enters a new degree of the zodiac in mid-winter at about the rate of every 21/2 to 3 minutes, and in summer at the rate of 3 to 43/4 minutes, that its magnetic influence varied the effect of the vibrations of ether waves of each planet, and so enabled these students of nature to carry their system in this way down to almost the smallest fraction of time.

Scientists, like Darwin in England, Flammarion in France, and others in Germany, made the startling discovery that there are actually tides in the solid earth itself, which are affected by the attaction of the moon. What then of the effect of the moon on the brain itself, which contains the most subtle essence and is one of the greatest mysteries known in life?

Granted that this be admitted, what then of the part

played on human nature by the rest of the planets, which are in each individual cases far larger than the moon ?

The following table showing the dimensions of each of the planets will illustrate that nay world I may use this side of the argument.

Diameter of mercury	2,000	miles
The moon	2,100	
Venus	7,510	
The Earth	7,913	
Mars	4,920	
Jupiter	88,390	
Saturn	71,900	
Uranus	33, 000	
Neptune	36,000	
The Sun	860,000	

I ask, is it logical, with such a demonstration before one to admit the effect of the moon and to deny any effect to the other planets that are in fact so much larger than it?

Let us now return to the important side of the question as regards the rules set forth in this book. You will very naturally ask, now and when were such numbers arrived at that represent the mechanical action or infuence of the celestial system on the people of this earth? I could write an entire volume on this side of the question alone, but in the following necessarily condensed pages you will find the general law explained which may be sufficient to elucidate the system contained in the following chapters.

In the first place, the secret or occult significance of numbers was revealed to man so far back in the world's history that the exact place of their discovery has never been recorded, but it suffices to state that if one goes back in one's investigations to the most distant period in the history of any race who made themselves in any degree responsible for such studies, even there one would find that these numbers representing the qualities of the solar system and the basis of all our later forms of calculation existed.

In working out the idea contained in these pages, I have carefully investigated every important form of occultism bearing on this question, but whether it has been Hindu, Egyptian, Chaldean, or Greek, the symbols of these numbers have always appeared the same their relation to months, days, hours, and people representing certain numbers, has been more or less alike.

What is called the secondary numbers' as illustrated on subsequent pages I myself have brought into a practical form, but they have in every case been built up from long investigation and experience extending over many years. Although we may never be able to find out the exact time in past ages when the influence of these numbers was discovered, that is no reason why we should not accept what has been given us by those ancient students, There are many other things we are forced to accept in life from being conscious of their truth, even when we are not able to get back to their birth or beginnings.

The origin of life we know not, but we are none the less

conscious that life exists. The balance, poise, and hidden laws governing our own solar system have also never been explained, together with a thousand other things in our everyday life. The very origin of number is itself a mystery: yet we are forced to employ them, and as Balzac says, without them, the whole edifice of our civilisation would fall to pieces'.

In the Book of the Wisdom of Solomon, now included in the Apocrypha, Solomon says:

For God Himself gave me an unerring knowledge of the things that are, to know the constitution of the world, the beginning and the end middle of times, the alterations of the solstices, the changes of seasons and the positions of the planets, the nature of living creatures and the thoughts of men, all things that are either secret or manifest I learned, for He that is the artificer of all things taught me this wisdom.

I ask, could anything be more forcible or convincing that such a statement, particularly when it is remembered that the true seal of Solomon was none other than the seven-pointed star which contained the nine numbers which constitute the base of all our calculations, and which is the root of the system of numbers as applied to human life?

Even in our chemistry we have given a number and symbol to all the elements.

Water is	1010 its symbol is H2O
Hydrogen	212 its symbol is H
Oxygen	1030 its symbol is O

Nitrogen	1969 its symbol is N
Carbon	1050 its symbol is C

And so on.

All occult studies point to the fact that the ancient students had foundation for ascribing to every human being his number in the universe, and if we admit, as we do, that there is a moment for birth and a moment for death, go also in the links of years, days, and hours, that make up the chain of life, it is not illogical to assume that every link of life has also both its number and place. I claim that by such a study man may become more perfect by his fitting in with the laws, system, and order of thins to which he ones his being.

There is evidence that those ancient students were conversant with the fact that there were two more distant planets than Saturn in our solar system, for they assigned beyond' the seven creative planets' the orbits for two more heavenly bodies, and they described them as governing the thoughts on the mental side of Nature and not the physical, and their description of them is in exact accordance with our present day knowledge of the recently discovered planet of uranns and neptune on human life.

The Planetary Numbers of the Months

Although later in these pages the reader will find how the single and compound numbers have each particular meaning in connection with human life, it is well at this stage to understand how and who the months have received their particular numbers.

The true solar year commences with the sun's entrance into the Vernal or spring Equinox on the 21st to the 23rd day of March of every year, and appears to pass through each sign of the zodiac of 30degrees each, one after the other, taking slightly under 3651/4 days in so doing, making our year popularly accepted as 365 days.

The Earth, revolving once upon its own axis each 24 hours, causes the whole of the 13 signs of the zodiac in their turn to pass over each portion of the Earth once each 24 hours. The moon revolves round the earth in a lunar month of 28 days. This wonderful mechanism, if I may call it so, is exactly like the hour-hand, minute-hand, and second-hand of a clock.

What is called the first sign of the zodiac is the ' period of the number 9' or the zodiacal Sign of Aries, from the 21st March to the 19th April. It is ruled by the planet Mars in its positive aspect and has the 9 for its number.

The 'period of the number 6 is the zodiacal sign of Taurus from the 20th April to the 20th May. It is ruled by the Planet Venus in its positive aspect, and has the 6 for its number.

The 'period of the number 5' is the Zodiacal sign of Gemini from the 21st May to the 20 June. It is ruled by the planet Mercury in its positive aspect, and has the 5 for its number.

The 'period of the 2 and 7' is the zodiacal sign of Cancer from the 21st June to the 20th july. It is ruled by the moon in its positive aspect, and has the double figure of 2-7 for its number.

The 'period of the 1and 4' is the zodiacal Sign of Leo, from the 21st July to the August. It is ruled by the sun in its positive aspect and has the double figures of 1-4 for its number.

The 2nd 'period of the number 5' is the Zodiacal Sign of Virgo from the 21st August to the 20th September. It is ruled by the planet Mercury in its negative aspect, and has the 5 for its number.

The 2nd ' period of the number 6' is the Zodiacal Sign of Libra for the 21st September to the 20th October. It is ruled by the planet Venus in its negative aspect, and have the 6 for its number.

The 2nd' period of the number 9, is the Zodiacal Sign of Scorpio from the 21st October to the 20th November. It is ruled by the planet Mars in its negative aspect, and has the 9 for its number.

The 'period of the number 3' is the Zodiacal Sign of Sagittarius from the 21st November to 20th December. It is ruled by the planet Jupiter in its positive aspect, and has the 3 for its number.

The 'period of the number 8' is the Zodiacal Sign of Capricorn, from the 21st December to the 20th January. It is ruled by the planet Saturn in its positive aspect, and has the 8 for its number.

The Fire Triangle

1st "House" March 21 to April 19.

2nd "Huse" July 21 to August 20.

3rd "House" November 21 to December 20.

The Air Triangle

1st House" May 21 to June 20.

2nd "House" September 21 to October 20.

3rd "House", January 21 to February 19.

The Water Triangle

1st "House," June 21 to July 20.

2nd "House," October 21 November 20.

3rd "House," February 19 to March 20.

The Earth Triangle.

1st "House," April 20 to May 20.

2nd "House" August 21 to September 20.

3rd "House, December 21 to January 20.

The 2nd 'period of the number 8' is the Zodiacal Sign of Aquarius, from the 21st January to the 21st February. It is ruled by the pianet Saturn in its negative aspect, and has the 8 for its number.

The 2nd 'period of the number 3' is the Zodiacal Sign of Pisces, from the 19th February to the 20th March. It is ruled by the planet Jupiter in its negative aspect, and has the 3 for its number.

This brings us back to the point from which we started. Owing to the Sun passing from one Sign of the Zodiac to another, seven days are allowed at the beginning of each sign and seven days at the end, which is called the 'Cusp of the sign; during this period the number of the month and the qualities it represents are not quite so strong as during the rest of the period, and partake to a certain extent of the qualities of the sign which is passing away with those of the one that is coming into action.

It will be observed that the planets have a positive and Negative quality in accordance with the period of the Zodiac they rule; the Positive giving the more physical and forceful quantities, the Negative the mental.

For example, the symbol of the 9 positive in the Sign of Aries is: A man in arm our with his visor closed and a naked sword in his hand.

The 9 negative in the Sign of Scorpio is represented by a man also in arm our, but with the visor up showing his face, and the sword in its sheath, giving the picture of the mental warrior rather than the physical.

The sun and the moon are the only two planets having what is called 'double numbers. Because the sun and uranus are interrelated one to another, so the number of the sun is written as 1-4.

The moon being interrelated with Neptune is written as 2-7.

A curious thing, and one well worth noting, is that there appears to be a sympathy and attraction between the numbers 1-4 and 2-7, and it will be found that persons born under any of the 1-4 numbers, such as the 1st, 4th, 10th, 13th, 19th, 22nd, 28th, and 31st, are sympathetic and get on well with people born under the numbers 2-7, such as the 2nd, 7th, 11th, 16th, 20th, 25th and 29th more especially so if either of these two sets of people is born in the "House of the Moon" namely between the 20th June and July 21st - 27th, or in the House of the Sun,' between the 21st July and August 20th -27th.

Note: I have added the seven days of he 'Cusp' to each of these periods.

The numbers given to the days of the week are as follows:

Sunday	1-4	Thursday	3
Monday	2-7	Friday	6
Tuesday	9	Saturday	8
Wednesday	5		

These numbers correspond to the Planets as follows:

Sun	1	Venus	6
Moon	2	Neptune	7
Jupiter	3	Saturn	8
Uranus	4	Mars	9
Mercury	5		

Root Number:1

English dates: 1,10,19 and 28

Persons born on dates 1, 10, 19 or 28 have 1 as their root number which is governed by the planet sun. Since Sun is the chief and lord of all planets, the number 1, represented by sun has also been considered as " Chief". High, better etc. Persons with 1 as their root number are illustrious, bold, hardworking and persevering . As and when Sun is strong and in transit such people will have a strong position in life. On the other hand a weak sun in transit would indicate troubles in the life of such people.

Weak Periods: The months of October, November, and December are roughly such when the sun's rays are not strong, hence this period is not much congenial to you. Setback in health, lack of interest in work, unnecessary worry and roaming is seen during this period.

Strong Periods: The strong position of the Sun in heavens will be considered to indicate the strong position of your life on earth. From this point of view the Sun has brilliant rays between 21st March and 28th April and between 10th July and 20th august. Hence these periods can be considered as conducive to your advancement and welfare.

Good Dates: All those men or ladies whose date of birth is 1, 10, 19 or 28 will be helpful and friendly to you. These dates also constitute turning points in your own life. Hence all actions started on these dates will be comparatively easy of accomplishment and success. High officials should be interviewed on important matters, important letters should be drafted, important new business should be stated on these dates to ensure easy success.

Good Days: Sunday and Monday in each week would give good results. If Sunday or Monday falls on any of the dates that are "good dates" for you that day will be more congenial and fruitful.

Good Colour: The colour most suited is yellow or copper colour. Golden yellow is even better than the yellow proper. You would be well advised to have in your drawing - room, curtains, covers of pillows and sheets etc. of this colour. The handkerchief of this colour is of course a must for you. In periods of ill-health it would be helpful to wear clothes of this colour .

Good Precious Stones: Your ruling stone is "Ruby" which is called Padma Rag in Sanskrit, Yakut in Persian, Chuni in Urdu. In auspicious time have a ruby of about 5 Ratties in weight embedded in a golden ring in such a way that it should touch the middle finger. The ruby should be fixed-in on a Sunday and the ring worn on the same day.

Health and Disease: You may complain of a weak heart or have one or other trouble connected with it. You may also be afflicted off and on by diseases of the blood. Blood pressure in old age, heart-attack and eye-trouble are likely to occur. You should give special care to the purity of blood and its proper circulation.

Fasting: If possible, you should keep fast on Sundays or take food only once that day. If you can avoid eating of salt (Sodium Chloride) on that day it would be still more helpful. On Sundays before meal, if you burn incense and recite "Aditya-Hridaya" you will feel, you have got rid or may obstacles and diseases.

Friendship: People born on 1, 10, 19 or 28 of any month or between 10th July and 20st and between 22nd March and 28th April, will prove more congenial, helpful and trustworthy. With such people you can have lasting friendship. Such people can prove helpful in business, partnership etc also.

Romance: Persons having 1, 4or 7 as their root number can prove helpful partners to you. You can enter into love relationship with such people ands be successful therein.

Your Traits: Your power of forbearance is excellent. You have been faced with terrible ups and downs in life and have been fighting constantly with opposing situations. In spite of these, there is no dearth of boldness in you, nor any sense of defeat. You have comparitively more vitality than others.

2. You have a strong disposition for leadership. You have been giving such leadership to your companions and friends in early age and to your colleagues in the advanced age. This is an inborn trait with you.

3. your circle of acquaintances will be wide. It is one of your special traits to make friends easily with unacquainted persons in a short time. You will be known to many in the society who will admire your actions and qualities .

4. Persons having I as their root number are always on the lookout for new things in life. It is their trait to do some new, and out of the way, feat or action in life. It is such people who leave some new legacy for posterity.

5. Your physical constitution is strong and robust which gives your ability to work physically as well without losing heart.

6. In business you will be a leader. The success of your business lies in your farsightedness, as a result of which you would be able to achieve much in comparitively short time. If you are in service you are likely to rise to high position commanding many persons under you. Whether it is business field or the social one, your leadership will be in evidence in both.

7. The greatest specially with you is that you have a distinct goal before you. You are fully alive to your goal and are steadily marching towards it instead of groping in the dark.

8. People with 1 as their root number are also clever in taking decisions. Indecision is nominal in them. The ability to take a quick decision in any work or business constitutes your success. Such a decision is generally right.

9. Independent personality, independent decision, independent life have been the main objectives before you.

You are incapable of working under threat. You are the architect of your own thoughts and schemes.

10. You are not happy with hackneyed practice. To add novelty to things will be your peculiarity. In office too. You will make use of new methods. Originality is a special and distinctive feature of your brain.

11. Whatever decision has been taken you stick to it. It is not in your nature to change your considered opinions or policies. For this reason you are trusted by the society and are considered trustworthy, efficient, honest, true and right.

12. The aggressiveness of ambition will be part of your nature. Your brain will always think as how best to rise high in life and get advanced. For this reason you may be occasionally irritated, upset and mentally unsatisfied but only for a short while, for in the next moment you are capable to throw away from your consideration such pessimistic thoughts and to engage yourself in constructive channels.

13. You desire the least interference in your work and you detest being objected to at every little step or being advised unasked for. You desire peace and you desire to make progress in the right direction.

14. To say that your brain is fertile for new thoughts, schemes or plans is no exaggeration. You are capable of becoming a successful "Planner". You will have growing contacts with new and good people.

15. Your labour to earn is matched by your liberality

in expenditure. You are spendthrift. You are not narrow of heart or mind. You are ready to spend where and when the occasion demands.

16. You love a life of beauty, of good tastes and good manners. You do not like disarray, laziness or slackness. You get a wife almost of the same thoughts as your own. You are capable of appreciating works of art and beauty.

17. You will hate flattery and false praise. Clear and to the point reply, appropriate to the time and place will be said to be your specialty.

18. You will have sudden income and expenditure. In other worlds there will be preponderance of unforeseen and sudden events in your life. You will gain and earn in sudden and unforeseen manner. Similarly, expenses will also be sudden and unforeseen. Occasions can arise when your budget gets unbalanced but soon you will be able to balance it.

19. You will have an influential personality as a result of which some of your work will be accomplished merely through the influence of that personality. Your personality is the cause of your success.

20. You will succeed in such types of work or business where a quick decision is essential, which brooks no slackness and which requires the exercise of good judgement.

21. You will be by nature clever, smiling and attractive. To attract people to yourself will be a chief trait with you.

Precautions: At times you spend more than is

necessary, due to a false sense of show. This is bad and the cause of an unbalanced budget with you.

2. The extent of being free of control increases beyond limits occasionally and thus proves a sign of danger for you.

3. You can take any amount of risk but you are advised not to take risks of financial character. This can land you in trouble.

4. Do not unduly trust any body. You have to be careful as even your relatives can deceive you in financial matters.

5. Beauty and attachment to women can bring you bad name. Hence the necessity to take well-considered and slow steps in such matters.

Good Dates: 1,4, 10, 13. 22, 28 and 31.

Good Years: 1.10,19,28,37,46,55,64 and 73 will be noteworthy years in your life. The total of each of the above years is 1. Hence all such years whose total is 1 can prove good welfare promoting years in your life.

Bad Dates: 7, 16 and 25. You should not start any important work on these dates.

Bad Years: 7, 16, 25, 34, 43,52,61 and 70 etc and all such years which total up to 7 cannot be said to be congenial or good for you.

Notable Personalities: Here is a let of leading and noteworthy personalities who had 1 as their root number:

S.No	Names	Born on	RootNo
1.	Alexander the Great	1July	1
2.	Duke of Wellington	1MAY	1
3.	General Gordon	28 January	1
4.	President Garfield	19 November	1
5.	David Livingstone	19 March	1
6.	Annie Besant	1 October	1
7.	President Wilson	28 December	1
8.	President Hoover	10 August	1
9.	Irwin Right	19 August	1
10.	Bismarck	1 April	1
11.	Capt. Coke	28 October	1
12.	Dante	28October	1
13.	Goethe	28August	1
14.	Meena Kumari	1August	1
15.	Rajendra Singh Bedi	1September	1
16.	Lata Mangeshkar	28 September	1
17.	Dr Sampurnanad	1January	1

Root Number: 2

English dates: 2, 11, 20 and 29.

The planet representing the number 2 is Moon who is emotional, gentle, fanciful and sweet tongued. According to the Vedic diction " Moon is born out of the mind-stuff of the Virat-Purusha" such person are of unsteady mind and cannot concentrate for long on any one subject, not can they persue an activity for long . New and yet new ideas strike them and new flights of imagination takes possession of their minds.

People with 2 as the root number are generally not of very sound physical constitution. But mentally such people are more healthy and strong. As a result such people prove more successful in mental vocations than in works requiring physical labour and exertion. They have a mind full of doubts. Such people work for the Welfare of others. They are seldom capable saying "No". "Yes" is always on their lips in every proposal or work. Being gentle in nature such people are merciful to others. They have a refined taste in beauty. In the fields of love and beauty they are past masters. They know the art of infatuating others. They can make acquaintances in no time. They do not hesitate to confess their mistakes. Due to lack of self-confidence they are often caught in arguments with their own selves. There are very frequent changes in their thoughts. To crow all the gentle and straightforward nature is prone to exploitation. Even when aware that the person opposite seeks his selfish ends by flattery: such people keep mum.

Because of being given to much fancy and imagination, they have to hear harsh words from their relatives. The inner mental clash goes on within them. Due to impatience wrong actions result, for which they continue repenting. Pessimism and inferiority complex also holds them, due to which they are often in morose and sad moods. Even though they have a good number of friends it is not possible that they should be benefited by such friends. They absence of real friends will always be keenly felt by them: such people can seldom remain without friends for long. Since such people need friends at every step their own work suffers in consequence.

Because of the lunar preponderance you are likely to womanish temperament and behaviour. In matters relating to women you will be lucky. Women will readily trust you and you will increase acquantance with them, comparatively more easily and soon. You may be an expert in taking work out of women and making them give out their secrets.

You have natural tendency to read the mind of other people. The person opposite may not speak out anything, still you are able to penetrate his mind an measure its depth. Much of your time and labour may be wasted as a result of your interest in fine arts. You will gain the confidence of your wife and will have the honour to be known as the husband of a beautiful and educated wife.

Your luck can fructify in cities adjacent to rivers, or the sea or places abounding in water. If works necessitating frequent travels are available to you, you can get hood profit out them.

Precautions: Although you are civilised, educated, cultured and a logical cultured and logical person, there are still certain aspect of life from which you should remain away in order to have better, more hopeful advance in life.

1. Have self-confidence. To lose heart at trivialities or suffer from inferiority complex does not become you

2. Whatever work you start, try to finish it. To leave the work midway in not proper to your personality. Whatever decision is taken, stick to it.

3. Take well considered steps in love matters, for in hurry you can make a bad curry of the whole affair. This can also lead to you bad name in the society.

4. Do not make hurry. Whatever the calamity or problem, think with a cool and claim mind on it. You will notice that doing so you do get a way out.

5. Do not increase the number of unnecessary and flattering friends. They are not your well-wishers.

6. Don't keep too much company of woman, nor increase intimacy with them, for this detracts from and does not add anything to your personality.

7. Don't take any decision of importance on full-mcon day, not go into deep water. For you the dark-half of the lunar

month is more conducive than the bright-half.

8. Similarly when moon is with Sun or very near it do not take any decision of importance.

9.To walk with the airs of woman, or to walk dragging the chappals, or to spread womanly smiles does not suit your personality.

Diseases: 1. Due to an emotional and feeling personality, your mind can be affected by even the smallest of event, condition or environment, hence there is fear of disease related to the heart,

2. You may also duffer from nerour troubles off and on.

3. There is likelihood of diseases connected with the digestive system. Dipepsia, want of appetite, constipation, intestinal troubles and gas complaints are other likely diseases.

4. There is the possibility of your death from pleurisy or any such other disease of the belly.

5. It behaves you to save yourself from infection.

Precautions: 1. Don't do any act that adversely affects your nervour system.

2. Neither come into contact with the patient nor be careless towards your won disease.

3. Get yourself vaccinated once in 6 months.

4. If you are weak, don't give in to excess of anger, for this can lead to swoons, loss of consciousness, coma etc.

5. Whenever Moon is weak in transit, you are likely to suffer from nervour trouble, cough, lungs complaints, etc. In such a state you take good care.

6. Have a stroll daily.

7. Don't brood too much or remain in a condition surcharged with emotions.

8. Don't do any work or endeavour or bring any thought which may increase your mental strain too much.

Weak Periods: Whenever, Moon traverses through the nakshatras of Sun i.e. Kritika, Uttaraphalguni and Uttarashadha or through the sign Leo or is with the Sun, these times will tend to adversely affect your health and give rise to mental disturbance. January, February and December are months that are not conducive to you.

Strong Periods: From 20th June to 27th July the position of Moon in the heavens is more congenial. Hence journey undertaken or auspicious actions started in this period is good for you and will lead to success.

Good Dates: 2, 11, 20 and 29th of any month are relatively more useful and good. 1, 4, 7, 10, 13, 16, 19, 22 and 25 are of medium goodness. Action done on good dates and at good time decidedly leads to success.

Good Days: Monday is the best week day for you. Fasting on full-moon day and the new-moon day will remove your worries and do you good.

Good Colour: Light green colour will increase your mental power. Snowy white clothes tend to increase your lustre and valour. Snowy white clothes tend to increase your lustre and valour. Grape colour is conducive to your nervous betterment and wellbeing. You should always have kerchief of white colour. Black, blue, green and purple are pain some and trouble-giving colours for you.

Good Precious Stones: Your ruling precious stone is pearl which is called Mukta in Sanskrit and Moti in persian.

The metal connected with you is silver. Hence to have pearls in a silver ring would work for your advancement. Pearly should always be clear, brilliant, soft and symmetrical. As far as possible pearls from Basra should be taken into use. The pearly ring should be worn in the middle finger. In case of disease, drinking water from out of a silver pot will help restore health quickly.

Friendship: Men and women born on 2, 11, 20 or 29th or a month i.e., those having 2 as their root number can prove to be your good friends. You can be benefited by such people. In matters like love business, partnership, social contacts and marriage etc., the cooperation of such people can give you success.

Romance: Men or women whose birth date is between 20th June and 27th July and whose root number is also 2 can profitably share in your secrets. Relationship with them can be sweet and confortable for long.

Good Years: Your life's 1, 10, 19, and 28th year are likely to prove beneficial. Similarly the years 37, 46, 55, 64 also are likely to lead to advancement in life. The years 4, 13, 22, 31, 35, 40, 44, 53, 62 and 71 can also be said to be years of betterment. The digit 7 is friendly to digit 2. Hence 7, 16, 25, 34, 52 and 61 years should also prove beneficial. The years 2, 11, 20, 29, 38, 47, 56, 65, 74 and 83 should prove the best years for you.

Bad dates: 5, 14 and 23 are bad for you.

Bad years: are 5, 14, 23, 32, 41, 50, 59, 68 and 77.

Draw your own conclusions by as through study of the above years and dates.

Notable Personalities. The following are the prominent and notable personalities with 2 as their roo number:

S.No	Name	Born on	Root No.
1.	Swedenberg	29 January	2
2.	Marie Antoniette	2 November	2
3.	Gladstone	29 December	2
4.	Sadi Cornot	11 August	2
5.	Napolean III	20 April	2
6.	Edison	11 February	2
7.	Ibson	20 March	2
8.	Charles II	29 May	2
9.	Thomas Hardy	2 June	2
10.	President Hardinge	2 November	2
11.	President Adams	11 July	2
12.	Joseph Jefferson	20 February	2

13.	Dilip Kumar	11December	2
14.	Sir Ashutosh Mukerji	29June	2
15.	Morarjee Desai	29 February	2
16.	Sumitranandan Pant	20 May	2
17	Harold Wilson	11March	2
18.	Herr Hitler	20 April	2
19.	Mahatma Gandhi	2October	2
20.	Mussolini	29 July	2
21.	Lal Bahasdur Shastri	2October	2
22.	General B.M. Kaul	2May	2
23.	Prophet Mohammed	20 April	2
24.	Mathura Das Mathur	20September	2
25.	Asha Parekh	20October	2
26.	Mala Sinha	11 November	2

Root Number: 3

English dates: 3, 12, 21 and 30.

This root number is indicative of power, boldness and strength. This is a indicative of power, boldness and strength. This is a number denoting solid labour and is a living embodiment of struggle.

Representative Planet: Number 3 is represented by the planet Jupiter who represents in addition to power, boldness and strength, also education, wisdom and religion. Such people are religious at heart but they are not tied to conventional religion. They are on the other hand flexible and good to al people. Jupiter has its place at the root of the first finger. Its stay in one sign is for 13 months. In Transit whenever Jupiter is eclipsed or afflicted by the Sun, People with 3 as their root number suffer in life and meet with failure. Similarly, whenever Jupiter during its transit is weak, such persons will also feel weakness in many spheres of their lives.

Time of Progress: During the period from 19th February to 20th March and from 21st November to 20th December Jupiter is strong and beneficial, hence these periods are profitable, Good and useful. New items of work, new business, new journey, new relations, new transactions, if initiated in the above period can prove more useful and successful. Hence you should start execution of new plans during this period.

Good Dates: 3, 12 and 21 st dates fo every month would be beneficial to you. Similarly the months of March, June and December will also prove beneficial. Meet higher officials on one of these dates. Write important letters so that they reach the high official concerned on the stipulated dates. Make such persons your friends and colleagues as have 3as their root numbers.

Bad Dates: Numbers 1 and 7 indicates sorrow and bad luck for you. Bad news from official sources will reach you on 7, 16 or 25th or a month. January and July and troublesome from the financial point of view.

Good Days: Mondays and Thursday are good for you. The results of other week days are ad under:-

1. Sundays - are indicative of failure, unnecessary arguments, losses, unnecessary travels, bad news, and trouble from government officials.

2. Mondays - are indicative of financial gains, contact with friends, good health, good news and favour from government officials.

3. Tuesdays - are indicative of mental Worry and disturbances heart burning and sadness.

4. Wednesdays - are indicative of financial gains, literary work, success in undertakings and fresh news.

5. Thursdays - are indicative of good news about relatives, gain from wife or the in-laws and benefits from official work.

6. Fridays - are indicative of luxury and ease, enjoyments, buying of new clothes and ornaments, meeting the lover of the lady-love, sexual pleasures and gains.

7. Saturdays-are indicative of substantial financial gains, betterment of prospects, specially heartening news and general comforts.

Good Colours: Yellow colour is special lucky for you. Purple, blue and pink colours are also favourable and useful for you. As far as possible you should keep in your pocket a handkerchief of yellow colour. If you have curtains of your drawing - room of purple colour, and the pillow-cases and sheets too of the same colour it would be very much conducive to your wealth and affluence.

Good Previous Stones: Yellow to page is the main ruling stone for you. It is called Pushparaj in Sanskrit. In Hindi it is called Pukhraj and Zard Yakut in Persian. This stone is available mainly in 5 colours.

i) Yellow like Turmeric

ii) Of the colour of kesar (Saffron)

iii) Of the colour of lemon

iv) Of the colour of gold,

v) White with slight yellow shade.

But for you yellow to page in best which should be

brilliant like gold and be also symmetrical in shape. This should not be less than 3 ratties in weight. It should be embedded in a golden ring and worn in the first finger. It should be so fixed in the ring as to touch the skin of the finger. Such a ring should be got prepared on a Thursday with Pushya asterism (nakshatra) and should be worn also the same day.

Physical Health: A Weak and afflicted Jupiter increases skin - troubles. It gives loose nerves and an uneasy mind, the private organ will be lethargic but the sex urge will increase. Be on the alert in regard to diseases with the blood and of the arthrities type.

Heart - trouble will be there n old age. It will also lead to consumption of tasty dishes, the tendency to eat something or other at all times, increase of flat in body, diabetes, septic, bite ever, heat eruption, colic pins and other belly troubles. If you are care less, you may suffer from jaundice, itching, skin-troubles, paralysis, hoping cough, etc. Hence you have to be very careful.

Fasting: You should fast on full-moon day. If sick keep fast on Thursdays. Recitation of Vishnu Sahasranam on Thursdays will also give you solace.

Friendship: You can develop friendship with such men or women who have 3 as their root number. Hence you should bear this fact in mind while entering into business partnership, business transactions, friendship contacts, love contacts etc. Apart from people having 3as their root number men or women having 6, 9, 15, 18, 24, 27 as their birth-dates can also prove your good friends.

Romance: Men or women who are born between 19th February and 21 March and between 21 November to December and those having 3as their root number can be partners in your life .You will soon succeed in establishing intimacy with such people.

Precautions: 1 You should be careful about food and should never eat in excess.

2. Keep away from the consumption of fatty substance.

3. Greasy food is not suitable for you.

4. Articles with sulphur content are good for your health.

5. Use as much of fruits as you can.

7. Avoid chilies and hot articles of food as far as possible.

Your Pecularities: No one can express the thoughts and feelings about yourself better than you. You know ell how to influence others and take out work from them.

2. Money does come to you but it does not sty with you. When money comes to you, you are in a way oblivious of all future, In times of want you easily become hopeless and depressed.

3. You have more than due element of selfishness. At times of need you will go to any length even to appease your enemy but when your purpose is served you do not take long to throw him off.

4. You will have high expenses. You will spend

particularly on luxury goods and articles of enjoyment.

5. Your ambitions are high. JA small position, a little money, small work, do not attract you. As you see persons with high status, you also strive to become like them.

6. You generally feel frustrated for when it is not possible to attain to your object of ambition. This is but natural.

7.You will desire a windfall or a sudden rise, but it would not be possible if you are not fully wide awake. You are responsive to social status and social conventions.

8. You will not benefit to any appreciable extent from brothers. Although due to your temperament enmity will not increase still there will be some ill-will, mutually leading to isolation

9. You do not interfere in the affairs of others. Nor do you like that others should interfere in your affairs.

10. With the acquisition of a little position or money you advance towards license. This is not good as license is one defect that spoils your personality. This trait of being self-willed gives rise to your enemies and creates rift among yourself and your friends.

11. You are wise, honest and liberal-minded and willing to lead a clean life but at the same time you do not raise your finger if money comes through unfair means, though afterwards you repent for it.

12. You get angry quickly. But the anger melts away as quickly as it comes. Even in the heat of anger you do not

let go discretion and wisdom out of your hands.

13. Quickness of speech, irrefutable logic, win over people to your side by sweet speech. This can be said to be your special trait.

14. You have for purposes of earning, more that one item of work at hand and are unable to maintain the requisite balance. This disorder sometimes is a possibility.

15. You will have many friends but friends will betray you. Hence be careful from this direction.

16. In the field of love you have in the main, to face failure. Even though you strive in this field and reap some benefit also, but lose your balance just before final success. Thus you miss success by a very narrow margin.

17. Your wife will be beautiful, chaste and loyal. Due to wife you will feel a sort of absence of worry.

18. Your childhood will be spent in ordinary manner but for education and you may have had to roam about.

19. In childhood you had not much of satisfaction nor did you get any substantial help from your family.

20. Horse-riding, physical fitness, official service are more pleasing to you. Even while holding a high post you are tied to a fixed routine and you wish to remain so tied up.

21. There are travels in your life and also profit from these travels. Whenever your feel bored you may undertake journeys. This will double your zeal and you will be able to have newer and newer experience.

22. If you desire promotion, you can have it through contacts. You are also likely to have contacts with high officials and V.I.P.s

23. In the matter of discipline you are hard and exacting. You are yourself a lover of discipline and it is your desire that subordinates and servants under you should also observe the rules of discipline like you.

24. You will have one or more of the following as means of livelihood - work involving law or one abounding in logic and argument viz. Professor, lecturer, teacher, social reformer, speaker or such other work where education is imparted through speech. Work connected with administration, press, publication of periodicals, publication of literary work, business, share-market, organizational work, leadership work or steadfast work, research work, work for enquiry, love or ancient history, politics, centre of industry, priest in a temple, reciter of mantras or religious work etc. etc.

25. In early age there will be less of fame, but as you reach the ripe age you will have earned full measure of name and fame.

26. Deep sleep, love for tasty food, hard labour, embellished house, and comforts can be side to be main pecularities of your life.

27. It is likely that you have a good conveyance soon after the 36th year of your life.

Warning: Don't engage your self in too much expenditure as you will there by entangled in financial imbalance.

2. Do not be jealous of others. by too much hurry you can neither become a millionaire nor a scholar.

3. You must save something, otherwise in times of the necessity you will find yourself alone.

4. Jealousy is your bitter enemy: avoid it.

5. Don't allow your standard of living to fall, nor should you keep low company.

Good Years: The years 3, 12, 21, 30, 33, 36, 48, 57, 66, 75 and 84 of your life will be nice ones.

Besides these, all those years which are divisible by 3 should prove beneficial to you. Similarly, the year of the century which are divisible by 3 should prove beneficial to you.

Skpecial: Your telephone, car conveyance, house etc. if these possess a number that is divisible by 3, will prove more beneficial. By careful not to buy a conveyance whose number is divisible by 7. Numbers friendly to 3 are 6 and 9.

Notable personalities: Notable and prominent people of the world who had 3 as their root number:

S.No	Name	Born on	Root No
1.	Lord Russel	12 August	3
2.	Abraham Lincoln	12 February	3
3.	Winston Churchill	30 November	3

4.	Charles Darwin	12 February	3
5.	George IV	12August	3
6.	Dean Swift	30 November	3
7.	Voltaire	21 November	3
8.	Mack Donals	12 October	3
9.	Sir Jagdish Chandra Bose	30November	3
10.	Dr. Narain Datt Shrimali	21 April	3
11.	Roosevelt	30 January	3
12.	President Nasser	21 January	3
13.	General Sam Maneck Shaw	3April	3
14.	Stalin	21 December	3
15.	Henry Ford	30 July	3
16.	Dr Rajendra Prasad	3 December	3
17.	Swami Vivekanand	12 January	3
18.	Aurangzeb	3 November	3
19.	Mehtab Chand Golchha	12 October	3
20.	Shammi Kapur	21 October	3
21.	Vimmi Kapur	21October	3
22.	Waheeda Rehman	3 February	3
23.	Pran	12 February	3
24.	David	21 June	3
25.	Rishikesh Mukerjee	30 September	3

Root Number: 4

English dates: 4, 13, 22 and 31.

The planet with most sudden burst is Herschel. This represents you. It has direct relation to the Sun. Sun himself is burning, Hot and billiant. Hence the scholars of Astrology have attributed the same traits to Herschel.

Herschel is particularly noted for creating ups and downs in life. Accordingly people who are under the sway of this planet i.e. those who have 4 as their root-number, are subject to ups and downs in life. There is preponderance of sudden events in their lives. In other words, Whatever good and beneficial gains, promotion, etc. That have come to them is sudden and unexpected. Similarly, whatever bad, and harmful, fall, expenses etc. comes to them also comes in the same sudden and in an unexpected way.

Such people do not belong to the middle. They are either on the highest ladder or in the deepest ditch. We have read and seen that a man of this type is now the President of a country holding the highest office and the next day he has been declared a conspirator against the state and is thrown behind the bars. Such events happen with the lives of people who have a dominant Herschel.

Pecularities: Your life is a life fo constant ups and downs and marked by struggles. In all types of work, howsoever small or great, there is always some obstacle. It is doubtful for you to accomplish any thing with out opposition or obstacles.

2. Herschel does not only represent your life as a whole but also controls fully your longevity and luck. Hence your advancement in career is also subject to obstacles and changes. Your temperament will be gentle than the Moon and severer than the Sun. In anger you forget everything. Personal loss often results to you for such anger. But anger goes away also as quickly as it arose. When the anger is gone there regret and sorrow at self-inflicted loss.

3. Suddenness is a speciality of your life. If your life. If you have to become a millionaire you become so in a few days but in the next few days you can also be under debt.

4. Although your life as a whole is full of ups and downs, struggles and labour, you nevertheless get opportunities of advancement in between, though you may not recognise them as such or take advantage there from.

5. Nothing can be said definitely about your temperament, thoughts, policies and plans. If you plan a thing in the evening. Your opponents get defeated on this very point.

6. You can keep things and matters to yourself and are capable of retaining secrets for ever because what you are going to do in the near future is beyond taken of not only

your opponents and relations but even wife.

7. There is no dearth of enemies for you. If you defeat one enemy ten more will crop up. Your enemies would conspire behind your back, will crop up. Your enemies would conspire behind your back, will create difficulties for you, will poison the ears of high officials against you and will leave no stone unturned against you, yet they will fail and will feel pale and defeated as soon as they face you. Thus the enemy can create nuisance for you but cannot harm you.

8. Though you know the art of making friends and you will make friends quickly too but soon the urge will subside. You will soon realize that the one you considered a friend has turned into an enemy and takes a leading part in conspiring against you. Hence you should be aware not from enemies but from friends.

9. You have friends mostly those who are leaders in some field, who have high calibre, whose anger is aroused soon and who are under the hot influence of planets like the Mars and the Sun. Your friendship will be intimate and thorough with such types of people.

10. Although you undertake work after due thought and circumspection yet you are instrumental for such actions Which turn bad in the future and result in loss to you. You also gain sometimes through such types of work.

11. You can take a quick decision. You think for hours on a problem but are unable to arrive at any conclusion. You are unable to decide whether you should or should not undertake a particular work. Nor are you able to estimate as to how much gain or loss you are likely to have through

your work.

12. On every problem, whether educational, social, political or individual you consult others and act according to their advice. To take an independent decision is difficult, if not impossible for you.

13 You are of aggressive temperament and this is the greatest hurdle in the way of your progress, for due to this aggressive attitude your admires turn into your critics. If you are boss in any office, then the subordinates under you are certainly afraid of you. Even though some people may be keeping you amused through false flattery, they will be foremost in turning tables against you at the first opportunity.

14. You known rules, regulations and the law but you consider it your right to break them. Hence you entangle your self in such actions at times. You are always cautions. But on occasions you are overcautious and turn yourself into man that in suspicion doubts every thing. You should perform some such actions, which instead of creating fear should create trust in you.

15. Selfishness is top-priority with you. You do not bother yourself if in gaining your selfish ends you harm others. But in life you will have occasions when situations will so comfort you that will realize that whatever you do, in whatever shape you do it, is not proper and is not in the interest of the masses.

16. At times you will feel isolated and sad. You will feel lonely and deserted, opposed by conspirators.

17. Do not spend unnecessarily. For progress in life it is essential that you should understand the importance of wealth and direct yourself towards saving it. You should spend what is necessary, and what is only absolutely necessary.

18. You are also showy - in the sense that you save little and show it beyond proportions. People remain in ignorance about it. People estimate your capital much more than what you actually possess. You hear it but do not contradict it, with the result that the misunderstanding instead of vanishing continues.

19. It is likely that you may have money unexpectedly. But if such a contingency has not arisen, you will have to work hard in old age and undergo undue trials and tribulations.

20. From out of the crowd of friends you do have a few who are fully sum pathetic towards you. They are truly trustworthy friends and by getting such friends you can really make your life happy and enjoyable. You do not give generally, but once when you decide to give, you do not go back on your words.

21. In truth, you are too quick and unduly intolerant. You desire that everything should be done expeditiously. You cannot brook delay, obstacle, or opposition to it.

22. With advancing age your power of memory will become weak. This slackness of brain is the result of your aggressive and angry temperament. This may even lead to similar trouble to posterity. It can come to your progeny. Hence it is essential that you retain control over yourself

and do not allow the brain to get heated or irritated.

23. The health of your wife will be weak. She will have some trouble or others relating to belly or the intestines. She can be operated upon as a result in rip age Wife will have an irritable temperament.

24. Control your heart. People with 4 as root-number have been observed to suffer from heart-trouble in old age or else they may suffer from a disease which is incapable of diagnosis even by doctors.

25. You have no love for arts. You will, however, take steps to show as if you are a good critic of the fine arts. At times you will visit music conferences, picture exhibitions and similar programmes.

26. You are not likely to be benefited from your father. You are likely to inherit paternal property in the first instance and even if you inherit it you will be faced with all sorts of difficulties and obstacles in acquiring it. You are rather to be benefited from brothers or relatives or from your sons. You will have sons but they will be rather a liability than as asset.

27. In your youth you will be faced with difficulties in ample measure, in securing a job or work to your liking. You will meet with obstacles in your academic career also. You will complete your education and rise in life more through the help of others than of your relatives.

28. You are not a person to stick to one line. You start a business and as soon as it begins to give profits you entangle yourself in another one. Thus you will have more

than one means of livlihood in life.

29. You are an aristocrat at heart. But on occasions when you have no money or your are in uncongenial circumstances your sight is pitiable. But no sooner you get some money in unexpected manner or through labour, you do not consider yourself less than an emperor and your expenses shoot up.

30. If you desire to make progress in life and honour in society you should learn to say "no" and a definite "no". To keep others in the dark, to give false promises and to say meaningless "Yes" is not proper, for the then you cannot finish your work which brings slur on your name. This is the reason why your friends turn into your critics.

Precautions: As far as possible keep cool. Keep a quit atmosphere in stead one of hue and cry. Do not do any act which may unnecessarily boil your blood.

2. Never censure others. If possible praise them.

3. Don't give false promises. If you can do a work say "Yes", also say "No" in uncertain terms. This will certainly add to and not subtract from your prestige.

4. Keep away from false "show". Cut your cost according to your cloth. Don't compare the living standards of others with your own, nor try to react or to imitate them.

5. Don't spend unnecessarily. Attend to the habit of saving and save something.

6. You will have relative shortage of blood. In old age there is the possibility or diseases of the blood. Hence take

care in this direction in time. Consult a doctor and so regulate your diet as not to fall a pery to blood trouble.

7. You should be careful about bad cold and other diseases of an in fectious nature, which you are likely to contract.

8. Keep away from animals, particularly horned animals, for you are liable to get injured by such animals.

9. Be careful in travels and do not blindly trust any body.

10. Be. Watchful of your growing age advancement of time.

11. Speak sweet and little.

Weak Time: In transit whenever Sun is in weak position, your time is not favourable. From this angle approximately October, November and December constitutes an ordinary period for you. During this period ther will be obstacles in the way of execution of jobs, set back in health, lack of zeal, laziness, unnecessary worry and laborious strings.

Progressive Time: The strong position of Sun in the heavens has been taken as the strong position of Herschel. Hence the period from 21st March to 28th April and from 10th July to 20th August is considered beneficial and conducive to power and advancement.

Good Dates: All such men and woman and women whose date of birth is 4, 13 22 or 31st will prove helpful and cooperating to you. These dates can prove a turning-point in your own life as well. All acts of importance initiated on one of these dates will undoubtedly lead to success. Select one of these dates for having an important interview with any high official.

Good Days: Saturday, Sunday and Monday are profitable to you. If one of these days falls one of your 'good dates' they can prove specially beneficial to you.

Good Colour: All type of shining colours - blue, khaki, gray - are favourable to you. Your drawing-room should depict one of these colours. If you have curtains etc. of one of these colours you are likely to be profited by it.

Good Precious Stones: Neelam is your ruling stone. It is called Indra Neel Mani in Sanskrit. Neelam in Hindi, Neelvil yakut in Persian and "sppitire Tuirgous" in English. Neelam should be of deep blue hue, of the colour of a peacock feather, shining, rather transparent, it should be approximately 6 Ratties in weight. It should be worn in ring of 5 metals on the middle finger. I have found in my personal experience that "Neelam" does not prove efficacious sometimes. In such an event Gomed of 6 Ratties should be worn by people with 4 as their root-number, on a Saturday on the middle finger.

Fasting: You fast on Mondays and on Ganesh Chaturthi. Fasting on Ganesh Chaturthi can prove benenficial to you in every way. On that day you shoul prepare "Laddoos" of ghee, gur and atta and offer them to Lord Ganesh before you take your meals.

Friendship: Men or women having 4 as their root number or who are born on 4,13,22, or 31 of a month, it contacted can easily be turned into friends. If you want to marry or see your love affairs prosper, you can succeed with such people-men or women - who are born between 21st March to 28th April or between 10th July to 20th August; for their root number too is 4. Such people can prove a boon to you.

Good years: People with 4 as their root number will have years 4, 13, 22, 31, 40, 49, 58, 67, 76 and 85 as best and beneficial years of their life. The years 8, 17, 26, 35, 44, 53, 62 and 71 will also prove significant. Main event of life will occur in these years.

In the opinion of some Western scholars, the number 1 is beneficial to persons having 4 as their root number. Hence years 1, 10, 19, 29, 37, 46, 55, 64, 73 and 82 can also be said to be the years of success. But in my personal experience this has not proved entirely true. Hence people with 4 as root number should verify and take their decision regarding the goodness or badness of these additional years.

Notable Personalities: Prominent and note-worthy people of the world who have 4 as their root number.

S. No.	Names	Born on	Root No.
1.	George Washingthon	13 April	4
2.	Lord Byron	22 January	4
3.	George Elliot	22 November	4
4.	Lord Beden Powel	22 February	4
5.	Farade	22October	4
6.	Prince Charles	31 December	4

7.	Francis Bacon	22 January	4
8.	Thomas Huxley	4 May	4
9.	Arthur Canan Doyle	22May	4
10.	Saint Augustine	13 November	4
11.	Kant	22 April	4
12.	Alexander the great	22 July	4
13.	President Rutherford	4 October	4
14.	Shri Ramanujacharya	4 April	4
15.	General Franco	4 December	4
16.	Seth Jamna Lal Bajaj	4 November	4
17.	Mohan Lal Sukhadia	31 July	4
18.	Vijayanti Mala	13 August	4
19.	Nutan	4 June	4
20.	Prem Dhavan	13 June	4
21.	Ashok Kumar	13 October	4
22.	Kishore Sahu	22 October	4
23.	S.D. Burman	22 October	4
24.	Jai Kishen (Music Composer)	4 October	4

Root Number: 5

English dates: 5, 14, and 23.

Five is a root number which we can call as full of thinking power. It is full of new arguments, modern thoughts, wonderful schemer and planner, with irrestible logic and unique understanding. It is a number with unique qualities. The man having this Number has a most active brain that is always busy thinking something or the other. He can bend but after bending his opponent with the weight of his logic. He can change his views but only after paling into insighificance his adversaries in argument. He can be robbed but only after he has expressed to his opponent and shown him all the points through his strong argumentative power. This is the root number of such men and women who are born on 5, 14 or 23rd of any month. The planet that represents this number is Mercury, who is gentle, high thinker, Pandit, scholar, given to amusements and striving after physical comforts of life. As a result persons represented by Mercury make people under them follow their thoughts. Hence all those men and women who have 5 as their root numbers are by temperament jocular and amusement-loving people. They have a fertile brain, mature thoughts and active in life. Such persons are always engaged in some activity or other. They know the value of time and put time to good use.

Representative Planet: You are represented by the planet Mercury, who is 36, 000,000 miles away from the sun and whose orbital motion is 88 days. The inclination of its acis is 7 degrees. It has an equatorial diameter of about 3100 miles. This planet is significator or "karka" or knowledge and science logic, astrology, astronomy and trade. People with 5 as root number are specially marked for their aptitude for trade. They may be in service or any other work but their inmost heart is in trade. Such people are a sure success if they engage themselves in trade.

Weak Periods: Lying as it does in between the Sun and the Earth, the planet Mercury is eclipsed many times during the year. Whenever this planet is eclipsed or in retrograde motion, is in transit it would not be conducive to people with 5 as their root number. It will lead them to situations involving houses in trade, financial crisis, mental worry, Weakness, physical trouble and unnecessary argumentation. You can fall prey to diseases of the skin, pollution of blood and meet with difficulties in your work. Hence you should exercise care, during such periods and should not enter into any trade agreement having far-reaching consequences. May, December and September are weak months for you, for during these months Mercury is somewhat weak. Hence keep control over your health during these months, exercise due care in trade transactions and be watchful or your financial interests. It is essential for you to be careful form both foes and friends.

Strong Time: Every action aimed at your progress should be started in strong time. New trade or business, business transactions, selling or buying of property and all other important work should be undertaken in strong time only. Strong time for you is between 21st May to 20th June and between 21st August and 20th September. This is the time of greatest benefit and importance that tends to boost your prospects. Hence make the best use of these periods.

Good dates: The dates 5, 14, and 23 in every month are suitable and favourable for you. Hence all important acts should initiated on one of these dates. If you can start act between 21st May and 20th June and between 21st August and 20th September, they are bound to lead to success and prove lucky. You should remember these dates as suitable for interview with high officials. In the execultion of the desired object write also in a way so that the letter reaches the quarters concerned that matter, on one of these dates viz. 5, 14 or 23.

Good days: Wednesday, Monday and Fridays are favourable to you. If these days fall on the "good dates referred to in the previous paragraphs these should be considered as specially suitable and favourable.

Good Colour: For you light green colour is lucky. White and gray are also favourable. It would be advisable to have in your hand a kerchief of light green colour. If you have curtain of the room, covers of sofaset and of cushions etc., also of the same colour, they will be still more conducive to your well-being and comfort.

Good precious Stones: Your ruling stone is Emerald

which is available in five colours:

1. of the colour of the feather of a parrot,
2. of the colour of green water,
3. of the colour of sharesh flower,
4. of the colour of a peacock,
5. of the light colour of Sandal flower.

You can wear Panna of any of these colours, but it should be devoid of defects, shining , transparent, brilliant and unbroken. It should be 6 ratties of minimum weight. It should be worn on the small finger on an auspicious day. A ring of gold or lplatinum goes well with Panna. Panna should be so embedded in the ring as to touch the skin. By wearing such a ring people have been seen to enhance their keen interllects, and to succeed in their undertakings. For traders, students and people in service "Panna" is a must.

Bodily Health: People under the sway of Mercury are easily afflicted by flue, bad cold etc. They are always prey to one or other trouble, as their skin is delicate, vital and soft due to which the microbes easily affect them, In early age too such people fall sick many a time and suffer severely one or twice in that age. Such people are capable of exercising their brains more than their muscles. As a result their nerves are always under constant pressure.

In advance age such people have been deserved to suffer from nervour troubles,. About sixty percent of people suffer from diseases of the brain as well. Headache, partial or complete and such other complaints remain with them constantly. They get their power of memory weakened and develop forgetfulness. They are also liable to blood pressure, weak heart etc. Diseases of the blood and skin always surround them. They should, therefore, pay special attention to the purity of their blood and should not undertake any work that may lead to commotion in blood. If neglected to far, they are liable at last to suffer from paralysis.

Precautions: 1. It behoves you not to remain in sad and morose surroundings, nor should you do any act which should bring about great regrets or sorrow or should put much strain on your brain.

2. Always remain in jovial environments and try to mix well with the children, laugh with them, play and dance with them and otherwise amuse, yourself in their company.

3. Go for a stroll in the morning and in the evening. The walk should not be far less than a mile.

4. Pay full attention to the purity of blood. Do not allow shortage to occur in the system of calcium and vitamins. Consult the doctor from time to time.

5. Be mindful about bad cold, flue and cold in general. It has been seen often that once you catch a disease, it does not leave you easily.

6. Do not read in the night and try to forget as far as possible the weakness of your heart.

7. Use salt i.e., sodium chloride to the maximum.

Fasting: You should fast on full moon-day and offer worship to Lakshmi Narain. Arrange for Katha fo Satya

Naraain and eat only once on that day. If possible avoid taking salt on Sunday. Eat only once on that day after giving Arghya to Sun.

Friendship: All men and women who have 5 as their root number can prove your best friends. You will be able to identify yourself thoroughly with such people and there will be no formalities between them and you. Such people should be selected for partnership in business or otherwise, marriage, love matters etc. as have 5, 14 or 23 as their date of birth. In selecting a partner in marriage you should ensure that he or she has his or her root number as 5 and is born between 21st May and 20th June or between 21st August and 20th September. If you get such a partner in life you are really lucky in life.

Romance: In this connection also you should bear in mind the requirements noted above. Give prominence to the number 5. People with root number 1or 3 can also share secrets of your life.

Four Peculiarities: 1. The greatest asset in your life is the art of winning others. After a very little time you are able to convert the other person to your point of view. Not only that he becomes your fast friend. As a result of this single good you do not feel lonely any where at any time.

2. Travels are in your nature and you derive pleasure too from travels. If you cannot have a travel due to busy occupation that is a different thing. This is, however, certain that every travel is to your advantage.

3. You possess a keen intellect. Your brain is fertile. You are expert in taking quick decisions being under the

influence of Mercury. You can judge the purpose of the visit of a person at his very sight i.e., what he intends to say. You can even anticipate through your fertile brain the nature of his query and your answer to it. To take decisions beforehand and in quick manner an be said to be a specialty of your brain.

4. The greatest quality in you is to be able to adept yourself to any situation. You are an innocent child in the company of children, a revolutionary youth with youth. Similarily you are a wise natured man when in company of the old people. Hence you are respected in every strata of society and your opinion is given due importance everywhere.

5. Even though you are spendthrift and can spend too much at times, still you are to control yourself in the matter.

6. Whatever work is done by you, you can put yourself into it all your heart and soul with no care for expenses. If any new idea or new plan comes to your brain, you engage yourself in it with all your heart and soul. At that time you do not mind other expenses or labour. This is the reason due to which you have risen to the position in which you find yourself at present.

7. You will not be satisfied with earning your livilihood through one line alone. You will have many types of business at a time. Your sources of income will be more than one to which you will be able to devote more or less. You will continue to exert. To sit idle is not in your nature.

8. You may be in any trade, vocation or service but your brain will be mainly trade-oriented. Your brain has the

special capacity to earn even from trivialities. You do not know dejection. You may have to face hopelessness in between and see even failure, but this will not effect your work. You will continue to work with the same speed.

9. You should enter trade whenever it is possible and feasible. You may start independent business or in partnership with some one, you are bound to succeed. Not only this even your partner in business will get his luck boosted through his contact with you.

10. In your life there are chances for getting sudden windfalls. Hence you are engaged in lottery, speculations or some such business. In your life you will have two or three occasions of heavy gains suddenly. In between you may lose even from your capital but this will not deter you from the pursuit. You will make up your losses by other means.

11. Only those succeed in life who take risks, not only take risks but be always prepared to take risks, not only take risks but be always prepared to take risks. In your personality this trait is fully embodied. Whenever you want and in whatever field you want you can take necessary risk, because your are ready to undertake new experiments. You have the ability both to make a correct assessment of a situation as also to wonderfully adapt yourself to them. The capacity to adapt yourself according to the time, person and situation is a significant specialty with you, a specialty which is capable of raising you to high positions.

12. In life, work is most important but you are fundamantally a believer in fate. You give to fate more importance than you give to Purshartha or endeavour.

Outwardly you may praise the Karma theory but inwardly you accept fate as more important. It is due to this belief and conviction that enables you to have equanimity in gains as well as in losses.

13. It is your good luck that you have been having helpers. If one helper or friend has turned his back another has taken his place. In short, to execute your plans you get at all times the requisite helpers, friends and allies. You have not felt dearth of real sympthisers in agreeable or disagreeable situations, through thick and thin.

14. You have special aptitude to grasp things. You are not dependent on servants, but try to understand yourself network or most intricate machinery or the intricacies and tactics of business and are soon expert in such matters. Soon then you lose interest in such matters and lines and take to new ones.

15. Your career will start in the 23rd year of your life. In the 34th year it will offer you more agreeable opportunity. There will be sudden gains in the middle of life by which you will be able to fulfil the needs and comforts of your physical existence.

16. Due to the care of the body you look young even in advanced age. Your constitution is capable of being put to severest strains. You can sue it over-time. Till death your body will not be flabby, worn out or weak.

17. When you make contacts with friends make them lifelong. Do not remove them in the middle, because your friends are your life's wealth, partners in joy and sorrow and instruments of your rise.

18. Continue your contacts with prominent people, lest they should form a wrong opinion about you. To meet such People without any selfish motive, off and on is a refinement of your personality.

19. Agreed that you have the knowledge of more than one art and you can speak with authority on any subject, you can even influence others thereby and create a soft corner for you in their hearts yet with all this you should not try to overwhelm them or to cut their arguments with your see thing criticism.

20. You make hurry by temperament. You are quickly irritated and regain your oldself again very quickly. This is not a very good thing. Before forming an opinion about any person, think seriously on points for and against him. Decision taken in anger will add to your prestige.

21. To give highest acceptance to one's own thoughts only is not proper. Listen to the opinions of others with patience and try to benefit from their experience.

Important Years: For people with 5 as root number the years. For people with 5 as root number the years 5, 14, 23, 32, 41, 50, 59, 68, 77 and 86 of their lives will prove beneficial, favourable and eventful. Besides, the years 1, 10, 19, 28, 37, 46, 55, 64, 73, 82 and 91 will also be favourable. Important events will happen in these years and you will move towards progress.

Notable personalities: Prominent and note-worthy people with 5 as their root number:

S. No.	Names	Born on	Root No
1.	Duke of windsor	23 June	5
2.	Lord Lister	5 April	5
3.	Shakespeare	23 April	5
4.	Thomas Hood	23 May	5
5.	Farenhieght	14 May	5
6.	Josephine	23 June	5
7.	Kari Marx	5 May	5
8.	Subhash Chandra Bose	23 January	5
9.	Queen Victoria	23 May	5
10.	Albert Einstine	14 March	5
11.	J.K. Birla	23 May	5
12.	Lokmanya Tilak	23 July	5
13.	C.D. Deshmukh	14 January	5
14.	C.R. Das	5 November	5
15.	Eishenhower	14 October	5
16.	Raj Kapoor	14 October	5
17.	Prem Chopra	23 December	5
18.	Kamini Kaushal	14 February	5
19.	Saira Bano	23 August	5
20.	Tanuja	23 September	5

21.	Gita Datt	23 November	5
22.	Krishan Chandar	23 November	5
23.	Shakti Samant	14 January	5
24.	K. Asif	14 June	5

Root Number: 6

English dates: 6, 15 and 24.

You are really lucky to have root number 6. All men and women bon on 6, 15 or 24th of any month have 6 as their root number. The planet that represents number 6 is Venus. In the heavens Venus is the most shining and brilliant of the planets. She can be seen as such even with the naked eyes. This planet has control over the sex urge in all beings and helps in the creation, rise and movement of semen and sex urge and power in the body.

The most beautiful women on earth have been under the control of this planet. In fact women who represent the number 6 are beautiful, symmetrical, attractive and have refined tastes. Men governed by number 6 are also full of youth and experts in sex matters. They are experts in attracting women towards themselves and in making them of the same mind. Such people are by nature, smiling, social, good mixers and clever. You have the adaptness of an actor precisely because your root number is 6. Such people are fully aware of the beauty around them. To become handsome and beautiful to the maximum extent is always their aim and endeavour. To dress nicely in most agreeable way, to be always in presentable shape, to decorate their place of residence, are the traits in such people due to the result of Venus. That is why you hate disorder, dirtyness, ugliness and mis-management. Such people are thoroughly meterial-minded. Their aim in life is to live a life of maximum comfort and luxury. Such people have a natural good critics of art, music literature, painting, etc. Their hobby includes one or other of the fine arts. They often spend lavishly as a result of this love of art.

Inspite of lack of finances they continue spending freely. They soon become popular with the masses and are able to extract form others there most guarded secrets. Material- minded, even grossly, yet they are clever and tactful. They think before they act. They weigh pros and cons of a situation and then act in an organized manner.

Such persons are long living, healthy, powerful, smiling and full of sex. Whenever Venus is strong and in transit movement such people feel an upsurge of sex and their aptitude for the arts increases. Wise and clever lovers succeed in getting their lady-love with relative ease at such times.

The married life of people with root number 6 remains ordinary. Even though such people respect the feelings of others and give. them due respect, yet they inwardly feel some sort of a shortcoming. It can be due possibly to the fact that there is the feeling of doubt in the mind of the beloved due to excessive love. Still from the surface there is no shortcoming observable in their married life. They bring together items and comfort and luxury in the home to the best of their ability and try to please their partner in life.

Such persons are temperamentally jealous. They may not be jealous as it were on seeing the progress of others, yet they are fired with a desire to surpass others. Sometimes this feeling results in adamancy, leading to unnecessary labour and expenses. If such people can leave jealousy and adamancy, they can live in comparatively more comfort.

Such people have the wonderful capability of influencing others. They do not hesitate to meet an unacquainted person or official. They place their view-point in such a manner that the other person cannot but say "Yes". Their symmetrical appearance, attractive body, gentle speech, charming personality, and gentle face unduly help them in all their undertakings.

To enter into argument is not part of their nature. From their side they do not allow any situation to arise that may lead to arguments and counter-arguments. If any situation involving a quarrel does arise they leave the field. A spirit of compromise is present in them from the very beginning.

Your Peculiarities. Apart from the pecularities mentioned above you have some other traits too which give your personality a sort of unique position.

1. You are rather usteady. You cannot concentrate on one subject for long, nor can you sit in one place for long. You prefer work involving movement to that which is sedentary in character. It is in former types of work that you are more successful.

2. Care of your dress and or make up of body is a

special trait found in you in ample measure. Someone may be waiting outside, you may be delayed from going office or even some important work is being spoiled, you will not leave the house till you have dressed yourself up fully and completely. When you are satisfied about your own person, then only you will handle any other work.

3. It would not be an exaggeration to say that fashions in dress have their start from you. These remarks apply particularly to women with 6 root number. New types of dresses, latest fashions, most modern and new embelishments, are owned and recognized by such women first of all. You are not only in the front row in fashions you are also foremost home. May be you are faced by financial stringency but no one can judge from your ways of dressing and make up that you are in such a stringency.

4. Your drawing-room is attractive and as far as possible fully equipped with gadgets of modern home comforts.

5. Fine sofa set, paintings ion latest use, radio, telephone, modern crockery and ways of living would be a part of your nature. You would not be able to part with them even if so willing. White clothes will suit you best. Even normally you would like to wear white. Smile be your invaluable wealth. There is some quality, some air some attraction in this smile which others lack. It is because of it that you can turn an enemy into a friend.

6. Inspite of all this, inspite of your being a good mixer, no one can easily guess your inner secrets. What is in your sleeves the next moment, cannot be guessed even by your wife, what to talk of others. You are on the other hand clever

in getting the secrets of others.

7. You cannot remain alone for long. This is your weakness. You would always like to be company of a friend or a group of friends. Loneliness will kill you. You will trust your friends more than others.

8. A feeling of despair soon becomes severe in you. A little action against your wish will make you despondent. You will soon lose heart and would try to get rid or that despair as soon as possible.

9. From the point of view of the family you can be said to be an excellent family man. To understand and appreciate the sorrows and joy of your wife, to give her solace and to slowly convert her to your own way of thinking are qualities that are natural to you.

10. Even being aloof towards parents, you will still remain sympathetic to them. You will be easily touched by their sorrow and will soon engage yourself in their service.

11. Beautiful women and handsome men will, in the main, come in your contact. To tolerate ugliness is beyond you. In sociability you will far exceed your relatives, friends and acquaintances.

Precautions: With whatever people you come in contact, you take them as your friends and readily trust them. This is not advisable as you have involved yourself thereby in many difficulties and have suffered in consequence. Hence you should learn to judge people on their merits and demerits and act accordingly.

2. You do not agree with others easily but start arguing

about it. It is your endeavour to prove your side as the winner and to defeat the opponent in argument logically. Even though this is cientific but this should not be universally applied. Where there is a thing worth agreeing to, it should be acknowledged as such. Otherwise this trait may prove an obstacle in the way to progress.

3. To act hurriedly in any matter does not become you. You should step forward only after understanding the whole matter slowly and steadily. Do not agree to the advice of your friends blindly, but take a decision only after testing it on the touchstone of logic and after due consideration of the likely losses or gains thereof.

4. In life do not give too much importance to women. You must have understood from your own experience that you have to undergo loss of wealth, time and labour by such importance, women is beauty. She is important also to your life, but don't allow love of women to exceed proper limits. This may lead to obstacles to your progress.

5. If you think over and decide to put in labour you can do so. In other words you have the ability to labour hard, but alongside with it there is laziness and luxurious tendency also in ample measure, under whose weight labour gives way. They result is slackening of the rate of progress.

6. You will have love affairs and will be attached to it, but you should ensure that this does not create any obstacles in the family life, for a small spark of fire can destroy the whole fabric of family life.

7.At times you feel like an upheaval in your family life. The cause underlying this upheaval is your aloofness towards your partner in life. To fall prey to somebody's love and thereby neglect your wife, cannot be said to be a good facet of your personality.

8. You will be popular in social circles and clubs. It is natural for you to be inclined toward them. These should not, however, usurp most of your time. Give them only that much importance which they deserve in life.

9. Intoxicant used only by way of fun may lead you to trouble. Hence wisdom lies in the fact that you should not use intoxicants at all. If you are accustomed of using one, get rid of it soon.

10. Sweet dishes and particularly special ones are your favourites. At times such inclination may exceed proper limits. Have control over yourself. From the point of view of health too much spicy food is also not conducive.

11. You are less angry. This is true. It is also true tht no body can guess your anger. But you are burning within yourself by the fire or revenge and would not rest until you have your revenge. But this leads you to sufferings at times. Hence you should be mindful of the upsurge of this spirit of revenge.

Health: You will have little complaint on the score of health. You will keep almost perfect health. Even otherwise you have the capacity to be unmindful minor complaints and do not allow people to feel that you have any complaint at all.

2. Most of your diseases would relate to the planet Venus. Whenever Venus is weak in transit, you will have

complaints in lungs, weakness of nerves, weakness of chest, urinary trouble, constipation etc. You can easily suffer from bad cold. If you are old in age you can suffer from phlegm and cough troubles.

3. There is favourable transit of Venus from 20th April to 21st May and from 23rd September to 20th October. This is most favourable time for you when you will not suffer from any ailment. Your face will have reddish hue and your whole body will appear spread out like rose petals.

4. As far as possible keep yourself away from intoxicants. In youth you can be an enjoyer of Bhang, wine and char as. This fun will turn into a habit and will give you trouble in old age. Hence if you exercise control over the intoxicants, your future life will surely be more happy and enjoyable.

5. You are incapable of digesting heavy food. Hence avoid heavy food as far as possible. If you use goats' milk in preference to that of buffalow it will be more agreeable to your health.

6. You should have a regular daily morning walk. This rule is conducive to the health of people with root number 6, because this will prevent constipation etc. Breath-control is also conducive to your health.

7. Your life is primarily one of enjoyment. You believe in the maxim, " Enjoyment is life". Still my advice to you would be that you save yourself from the strong urge of enjoyment as far as possible. For you to remain healthy, handsome, strong and attractive this control is not only necessary, but very necessary.

8. Avoid as far as possible the use of too hot things, spices, chillies, oil, sour things and much salt.

9. Organize your life. An artist is admired best as an artist. But to remain an artist at all times is not proper. Instead of idealism and pure emotionalism you should try to bring in some practicability. Then alone will life be happy and praiseworthy.

Precautions: Although you are alert, you need to care for some things and try to apply them to life. You will have to admit that physical labour is not within your power. Hence you should not start any scheme which requires physical labour. On the other hand you can put in more mental labour which are also likely to be more successful.

2. Whether you are in service or business your mind will be more or less directed towards luxurious enjoyments. The cause of it is Venus. Hence the following items of work can make you a rich person, a millionaire:

a) Trade in articles of beauty, (b) shop of articles of daily use, (c) partnership, (d) work as commission agent, (e) shop of luxury, ornaments, akis to beauty etc. (f) Publication or editing of books and film journals (g) trade in white articles.

3. Work connected with mines, construction work, contract work, painting, literature, goods connected with music can also serve as instruments of your livelihood.

Weak Time: April, October and November of a year are not good months for you. In these months mental worry are obstacles are likely and you may hear unwelcome news.

From the health point of view these months cannot be said to be agreeable.

Strong Time: Time from 20st April to 18th May and 21st September to 29th October can be said to be hopeful. Along with it the period from 20th to 30th April and 1st to 19th October should also be considered as good provided transit position of favourable results and advancement.

Good Dates: People having 6 as their root number have 6, 15 and 24 dates of all months favourable and profitable. Dates divisible by 3 such as 3, 6, 9, 12, 15, 18, 21, 24, 27and 30 can also be said to be favourable. New works should be stared on any one of these dates. These are also suitable for interviews with important officials.

Good Days: Wednesdays and Fridays are good and favourable. If one of these two days falls on the good dates also, the combination is more favourable.

Good Colour: Light blue, pink, ordinary yellow and shining white are highly beneficial colours for you. It would be more powerful in effect, if you have covers for your sofa sets, bed sheets and curtains also of these colours. As far as possible wear white. In white clothes your personal influence will increase manifold.

Good Previous Stones: You are a person having Venus as prominent planet. Hence your precious ruling stone is Diamond the best of stones. In Sanskrit it is called Vajramani or Indramani. In Hindi it is called Heera and Almas in Persian. The bigger the diamond the more useful would it be for you. Have it embedded in a golden ring which should be worn on the small finger. In fact this precious stone gives quick results, increases power and attraction and serves for all round progress of people with 6 as their root number.

Friendship: People with 3 or 9 as their root number can prove to be your fast friends. Friendship of such people is also profitable. In business, in partnership, in companionship, in selecting a partner for marriage or while keeping a servant these numbers should be kept in mind. Besides, men and women born between 21st September and 19th October and between 21st April and 18th May can also prove trustworthy and favourable to you.

Good Years: Your root number being 6, years 6, 15, 24, 33, 42, 51, 60, 69 and 78 of life can prove more favourable, profitable and turning points in life. If you would examine, you would find that the years 3, 6, 9, 12, 15, 18, 21, 24, 27, 30, 33, 36, 39, 42, 45, 48, 51, 57, 60, 63, 66, 69, 72 and 75 have also or will prove profitable and favourable. All western years which are divisible by 6 can be said to be lucky for you. Form this point of view the years 1974, 1980, 1986, 1992 and 1998 can be said to be favourable years for you.

In Fact you are lucky and one of those who are even born in ordinary homes rise to high position, who do not shine themselves, but also lustre to the name of the family and earn lasting and astoniship fame.

Notable Personalities: Prominent people with 6 as their root numbers:

S.No.	Names	Born on	RootNo.
1.	Queen Victoria	24 May	6
2.	Napoleon 1	15 August	6
3.	Oliver Cromwell	24 April	6
4.	President Traft	15 September	6
5.	Sir Walter Scott	6 December	6
6.	Sir william Herschel	15 November	6
7.	Warren Hastings	6 December	6
8.	Max Muller	6 December	6
9.	Admiral Perry	6 May	6
10.	Tennyon	6 August	6
11.	Dalai Lama	6 June	6
12.	Changez Khan	15 December	6
13.	Aurovindo Ghosh	15 August	6
14.	Akbar-the great	24 November	6
15.	Joy Mukerjee	24 February	6
16.	Jyant	15 October	6
17.	Manoj Kumar	24 July	6
18.	Prithviraj Kapoor	6 November	6
19.	Sheikh Mukthar	24 Dec	6
20.	Sajjan	15 January	6

21.	Indira	6 March	6
22.	Saiyeeda Khan	24October	6
23.	Mohd. Rafi	24 November	6
24.	Talat Mehmood	24 February	6
25.	S.D. Burman	6 October	6
26.	Pradeep	6 February	6

Root Number: 7

English Numbers: 7, 16 and 25.

Your root number 7 is a watery root number which is prominent in compassion, tolerence and cooperation. The planet ruling and controlling you is Varuna or Neptune, which has a diameter of 33 thousand miles and which is next to Saturn in influencing people on Earth. Being away form the Sun it is a slow-moving planet and takes many years in traversing a single sign. Hence its influence too is deep, comprehensive and long-lasting.

In Hindu Shastra Varuna has been considered as presiding over water. That is why I have called in it a watery-Planet. Following its own temperament, this planet makes you of fool temperament, content, tolerent, gentle, straight forward and imaginative. Imagination is its chief trait. Hence all poet, Philosophers, scientists who by their work have make the world more civilized, progressive and worth living, have surely been influenced more less by this planet, It is your good luck that you are influenced and controlled by this planet. Surely this planet will make you revel in water and will also offer you opportunities for water travel, Travel by sea and by air will be carried out by you once or twice in life. Your brain is original and fertile, as a result of which you are thinking about one or other of the new plans. In the house, you would try to break up obsolete things into new and useful things. Your brain does not consider any thing to be useless. You know how to put everything into advantageous use.

If you are a writer or a poet, then no sooner there is a favourable transit of Neptune, it will make you write a book that will boost your fame and personality manifold. The book will also have such specialties as will attract people towards you. If you have powerful spiritual make up you will surely be a prominent, yogi and philosopher.

Another thing that has come to my personal experience is that Neptune people are generally very successful and lucky. It is possible you may be rich at present or you are being tossed by troubles and it appears as if you are not making progress at the desired rate, yet if you examine in detail, you will find that you are still lucky on the whole. In regard to your family environment an circumstance, you will notice that you have crossed many a milestone which an ordinary person is incapable of crossing. Your contact also makes the other person lucky. When you break friendship with a friend you will notice his progress is thwarted after such a break. Similarly, if you are serving a boss, he becomes lucky because of you . Basically you have three qualities. First is originality. A thing that you dislike is really not good. It needs being reformed in some way or the other. If you make up your mind you will surely not rest till it is reformed or mended. Similarly, things which are considered useless by others will be but to some use or other by you through investigation. The second quality is "Power or Independent Thinking". Every moment you are thinking on something or the other. Your brain cannot be empty or idle. Its thinking has some substances or the other. Besides, you are a great champion of personal liberty. In your office too if some one is treated unjustly you will be the first to jump to his help and espouse his cause. You may even enter into arguments with the official concerned but cannot see any liberated being trampled upon. You may not be a successful speaker, but surely you are a successful creator of appropriate contrivances. You present your case in a what that the opponent has to agree to. Your third prominent quality is broad individuality. Your field of acquaintances will be wide. Officials higher in status than you will also be acquainted to you. Although you are gentle, you cannot work under threat of any body. Your acquaintance with the high officials will be one of equality and not one as between a master and a servant. You do not pay attention to trivial mistakes. If you hold an executive post your treatment towards your subordinates will surely be cordial. You may appear hard on surface but inside you are as soft as wax and this constitutes your broad individuality. In society you will be looked upon with respect. Although your are busy most of the time, yet whatever time you get as spare, you will spend on social activities. Hence you will continue to be important in the eyes of society. Ordinary people will approach you with their problems an you will be able to give a decision in a manner which both the parties will consider as just and be satisfied with it. You cannot be called of a set temperament. This changeable temperament will make you progressive and won't allow you to become dull or inert. You will be counted as a child whit children, a youth with the youth and a wise man with the old people. You will have the wonderful capacity to mould yourself according to a particular environment. Due to this, you will continue to be popular with every class of people.

Those who have 7 as their root number have the wonderful intution to know the mind of the man to whom they may be talking. All people are more or less of this power. If any person comes to you in home or office, you can at once guess, why the visitor has come, what is he going to say? Before he asks any question you are ready with the answer.

You cannot, therefore, easily be deceived. In truth, you work under your own direction. You do take the advice of many people if a problem arises: you discuss it with many persons, but ultimately you do that only which you think best and on which you set your own mind. Taking the counsel of others has the benefit of giving you the lines of thinking of others and to what length a particular person can be of help to you. Thus you are able to decide the likely result of action under execution. Thus no planning of yours goes in vain.

You will order people the least. If, however, once you tell them to do a particular piece of work, it will be you desire to have it completed within the stipulated limit. You would also desire it to be completed in the manner in which you desire it. Your orders are disregarded the least.

Once a person meets you cannot forget you easily, You have a very good memory too. Its cause is your magnetic personality which cannot be forgotten by others. Your personality leaves such impression on the minds of people that have a long lasting impression.

You get the cooperation as will as profit from your friends. During the early educational period of your life you have had a friend who was devoted to you from the very core of his heart.

He would prove useful to you not only in boyhood but in youth as well, so much so that you will not be able to disregard him in times of calamity. Although it is also true that you have had such friends also who were selfish and opportunists, still from amongst such a coal you are sure to have had come across some real diamonds which prove invaluable for you and would prove so in future as well.

You would have adventurist bent of mind. Literature containing situations that make the hair stand on end would be to your taste. You have been heartened by literature dealing with spies that take risks of their lives or with patriots who would risk their all for their country. Your natural inclination is towards such a literature. This does not, however, mean that you would turn your face to other types of literature. Fact You are aware to some extent about every type of literature and you would be able to speak on any topic with authority.

From your childhood you have had a strong desire for extensive travels, including travels abroad. You will be studying matters relating to other countries for maximum knowledge about those countries. On seeing mountaneous regions and natural scenery etc. Your .hair stand on edge naturally. But you should not approach deep water to tease and cajole your friends while bathing. You should also be careful not to race with any one in water and thus approach deep waters.

Your Peculiarities. You are brave. You are prepared to take greatest risk at all times. You are not aware of this latent trait in you character. You would do better to recognise it.

2. If you are a trader, establish your relations with foreign countries and try to expand your business in those countries. This is the way for the rise of your luck. Try to advance on this path without fear.

3. Although you are hardworking, yet at times your hard work goes in vain. It is because it is only the hard work carried out in the right direction that is profitable. You should clearly understand that your luck is to rise through business and business also of a specialised kind, comprising iron and electricity. In other words to manufacture electrical goods or to sell such items, as spare parts of machinery can be said to be most favourable for you.

Precautions: While you have some special and rare qualities you have also some weaknesses too. If you can overcome these weaknesses you can undoubtedly make headway. It is good to carry out well-being of others and it is also good to help others, but to be entangled in excessive emotionalism does not become your personality. He would do you good if you think what you are going to lose or gain.

2. Neither enter deep in the waters of a river, pond or a reservoir nor race towards deep waters.

3. It is true that your brain is fertile and is active in

working out new and basic plans, but it is not true to say that you can change your opinions soon. To change opinions so often is not the mark of a good personality.

4. Along with mental labour you should also put in physical labour as well. So long as you avoid physical labour your rate of progress will be slow. Hence to waste time is not proper for you.

5.To disregard opportunity or not to recognise it is your greatest shortcoming. By spending time purely in amusement or gossip you only harm yourself and none other. Hence recognise the value of time and take full advantage of it.

6. To depend on others is not proper for you. As far as possible, try to be self-sufficient. If you are a partner in business try to be independent in order to be able to rise to some being and to present to the world something worthwhile.

7. This is almost certain that you would head towards affluence after the 34th year of your life. As and when time passes thereafter you will become a prominent and rich person. But be careful not to be intoxicated too much by wealth.

8. You always profit when you do any work with awareness, alertness and devotion. You should also remember that if you are a little non-alert or relaxing, this can also lead to much more loss too.

9. Your life is not static but dynamic. Life will present occasions for profit as well as loss. Hence beware of the ever-Changing pattern of the world, lest you should be

responsible for converting your gain into loss.

10. It is true that you are progressive and are in step with the times and are not a prey to blind belief, blind worship or superstitions, but to always laugh at the forefathers or to bitterly criticise religious affairs does not become you. You should be more and more tolerant.

11. Behave with your wife as a friend. Neither consider her as a bought slave nor disregard her thoughts. Do not compare your wife with the wives of others. As far as possible make your wife aggreable to you by a slow process, It will make your life more happy and prosperous.

12. It is not in your power to within the four walls of your house, nor are you very much interested in domestic affairs, for your mind is always in travels. But it should be called your good fortune that you have domestic problems. Is it proper for you to disregard such a wife? Is it proper for you to return home late hours? Try to change and reform yourself in these matters.

13. It is possible that because of too frequent travels, you may not be attracted towards them, in between. But be assured that your rise in life lies in travels. Every such service, trade or occupation which is related to travels will be lucky and profitable for you.

14. Do not put your hand to any work in hurry. Whatever you may desire to do, get practical knowledge about it in the first instance. Try deeply to understand the pros and cons of it before starting it. Control hurry in your temperament.

15. It is not in your interest to work on commission basis. You start your own independent business. If you have

to serve, serve in some private firm. In this way you will soon be able to move to progress.

16. As far as possible, keep in your house some flower pots that are green in colour. Have a look at them soon after leaving the bed in the morning. You will feel refreshed by coming into contact with nature in the morning and you will pass a happy day.

17. Your face is gentle. Your eyes are big and watery which can easily win over people. Hence you are capable to make your own any person at the very first meeting. Women who have 7 as their root number are surely beautiful, graceful, sweet and endowed with charming personality. There is not the least doubt about it.

18. You should understand another point. You may come into contact with many women, but you are not lucky in the matter of love. The fruit of love is spoiled before it matures with the result that in despair you have to start the whole thing de novo.

19. Don't undertake any work that is beyond your capacity; for there is fear of your losing the importance of your personality. Cut your coat according to your cloth. Too much hankering does not become you.

Health: You will suffer from infectious diseases of and on. A little contact with infection will easily make you a prey to the infectious germs. Hence keep your-self away from such type of people as far as possible.

2. Your skin is soft and delicate. Due to the watery constitution of your body you will have plenty of

perspiration, you must use soap in your morning bath. Otherwise the bad smell from your body will have to be tolerated by you along with others.

3. The constitution of your digestive system would be such as to often give you indigestive system would be such as to often give you indigestion. Greasy food is not suited to your nature. Hence take simple food is not suited to your n nature. Hence take simple food. Don't allow constipation to occur. You would be generally worried from diseases belly.

4. You will be attacked now and then diseases of the private parts, gout in old age, grow and arthirtis, etc. Don't allow the disease to kill it in the infancy.

5. You will weakness as a result of luxurious living. Hence control your life from the very beginning. Neither indulge in too much enjoyment nor be unmindful about your physical weakness.

6. Blood troubles will worry you off and on. Hence at the time of change of season, better have your stomach cleared Take Triphala powder regularly.

7. After 40 years, power of memory will tend to become weak. Alongside you will have increasingly phlegm, cough, blood trouble, perspiration, palpitation etc. After the age of 50 it is advisable not to be careless about blood pressure.

8. You should always use such articles of food as have plenty of Vitamins A, D or E in them, so that your constitution can successfully face diseases and keep you fit.

9. Use fruit juice as much as you can. Fruits growing in water such as Singhara should be your most cherished fruit.

10. Save yourself, as far as possible, from smoking, for you can suffer from weakness of lungs and heart. In such circumstances, use of tobacco, smoking or other intoxicants is not to your advantage.

11. It is a special trait of persons with 7 as their root number that they can easily concentrate on a point. You should practice concentration. Slowly, when concentration is established you will experience strange phenomenon. You will see that the impression of many an event that are likely is focused on your sight. You will then be able to see the future about a person by the mere sight of it. Hence such practice of concentration is not only conducive to your own health, but is also instrumental in your material prosperity.

12. Whenever you feel worried or are fed up with engagements or find yourself in a fix, you better go far away to the bank of some river or a waterfall, to mother nature. This will give you mental solace as well physical energy and refreshment on the other.

Weak Time: In heavens whenever the planet Neptune is weak in transit, the time will be ordinary for the success of your undertakings. Hence you should observe care during the months of January, February, July and August and avoid, as far as possible risky undertakings then. Besides, you have to pay special attention to your health in these months.

Strong Time: In heavens, whenever, the planet Neptune is strong and in transit, the time would be indicator of your success and progress. You will stand to gain, if you start any new business or selling and buying transactions in such a time The month of June can be said to be barbinger of progress for you.

Good Dates: Your root number being 7, the dates 7, 16, and 25 in any month are beneficial and promoters of happiness. Number 1 is also your friend, and hence beneficial to you.

Good Days: Sundays, Mondays and Wednesdays are favourable days for you. If at initiating and undertaking there is a combination of good time, good day and good date, that day can be said to be excellent for you.

Good Colour: White colour suits you much. But light blue is still more suitable and promoter of good. Hence you should generally wear white clothes. In the home use of light blue curtains and covers of cusions and beds can prove more effective.

Good precious stones: The main ruling stone for you is 'Cats' eye stone"- also called Lashsunya in Hindi, Sutramani or Vaidurya in Sanskrit and Vaidur in Persian. In this gem there are small white lines. This is the criterion for the recognition of a good " Cats' eye stone". The best Cats' eye stone should not have more or less lines than two and a half in it. This gem is found mainly in four colours.

(1) Yellow like adried leave, (2) Black, (3) Green and (4) White with Green. White or yellow one is best suited to you. If you have it embedded in a golden ring and wear it in the small finger, next to your skin you can easily have all items of comfort easily.

Friendship: Men or women who have 7 or 1 as their root number, will all prove your true friends. People born on dates 1, 10, 19, 28, 7, 16 or 25 would prove most trustworthy in friendship and otherwise helpful. Besides, persons born in January or February on the above mentioned dates are still more sure to prove not only agreeable but helpful to you.

Good years: Your root number is 7. Hence years 7, 16, 25, 34, 43, 52, 61, 70, 79, 88 and 97 are lucky and promotion giving years for you. If you examine you will find the years 1, 10, 19, 28, 37, 46, 55, 64, 73, 82 and 91 also as having proved favourable to you, so also are years that are divisible by 7. From this angle the years 1974, 1981, 188, 1995 and 2002 are rich and lucky years for you.

In reality your courage is praiseworthy: that even amongst the calamities, opposing situations and struggles you are piloting your ship of life without extraneous help and are progressing.

Notable Personalities: Prominent and noteworthy personalities having 7 as their root number:

S.No.	Names	Born on	RootNo.
1.	Queen Elizabeth	7 September	7
2.	Sir John Franklin	16 April	7
3.	Poet Browing	7 May	7
4.	William Wordsworth	7 April	7
5.	Shyama Prashad Mukerjee	7 July	7
6.	William Marconi	25 April	7
7.	Atal Behari Vajpayee	25 December	7

Root Number: 8

English dates: 8, 17, and 26.

The Number 8 is considered in Astrology as the "number of confidence". This number has very control as it is governed by the planet Saturn. Saturn remains in each sign for about 21/2 years and completes its revolution in about 30 years. Out of the 9 planets, Saturn alone is one, whose revolutionary period is the longest.

It is your good fortune that your life is under the control of the saturn and he is governor of your temperament. Saturn is so intricate a planet that to properly understand it is difficult even for the experts in astronomy. In the same manner your life too is full of ups and downs are terrible struggles. It is difficult to say which event may take place, when your life will be so full of changes that it would be difficult for people to understand you fully. IF they claim that they have understood you, they are wrong. To guess your mind from your face is one of the most difficult tasks and what you are going to do the next moment is beyond the ken not only of others but even your nearest relatives, including your wife.

You are of a meditative nature. You go on with your work without creating any noise, without self advertisement or without beating drums, but such work is not shallow but solid from inside. Whenever such a work comes to the public notice, the people are wonderstruck and cannot refrain themselves from paying you a fitting tribute.

You are grave by nature. There is no childishness in your life, nor can it grow in your life. Whatever you would say, would be based on solid proofs and on the solid foundation of experience. People will not dare to disregard your word in light vein for they know that your word is always trustworthy and authoritative. This grave temperament is useful to you, but it has some disadvantages as well. It is useful in the sense, that in this way you are able to save sufficient time, in which you can carry out your important and solid work. But the disadvantages are that there by you are isolated from society. Your life becomes lonely in a way. This is all the influence of Saturn and you cannot change your temperament in this regard.

In astrological field saturn in an "Airy" planet and for that reason the effect of "Air" element on your life and personality should be taken as prominent. Air, when it flows, slowly gives pleasure to people but when it takes the form of a severe cyclone, to becomes so terrible that even the mighty start trembling. In exactly the same manner acts your personality. For so long as you are an ally and helper to somebody, you serve him in every way and act as a shield for him, may give him shelter like the shade of a banyan tree, but when you are angry with some body or are inimical to someone, then your personality takes the form of a severe cyclone and you make up your kind to finish him. You create in your mind such severe enmity that you do not rest till he is defeated. Hence few can face your destructive attitude, though this attitude is seen only occasionally. " Middling" situation is almost absent from your life. When you gain, the gain is of a very high order, but whenever, Saturn is eclipsed, retrograde or afflicted, you will have to face, a calamity under which others in your position would give way. But you will again take the situation under your control in a few days.

As I have said before, you are cool, gentle and a lover of solitude. Too much joke cutting, gossips or whiling away time is simply intolerable to you. Hence there is very little of window-dressing in you. If we may call you a silent thinker or a silent worker, working far away from propaganda, it will not be an exaggeration.

Stiff outwardly you are inwarldy very soft. Even appearing hard like a rock, you have a soft flowerlike heart. Your mind is soft like the butter and is even anxious to getlove. Not everybody but only one on whom your shower your love can see yor soft and innocent heart.

You are friend of friends. Even though people will generally fail to understand and appreciate you and even otherwise too, you will have very few friends in life, but once you make someone your friend you are ever ready to sacrifice everything for him. You will bear loss yourself, you will undergo hardships yourself, but will not allow any harm to come to your friend. This is the beauty of your personality.

You do not like exaggeration not anything of low taste. You will never be satisfied in life with small and low deeds. It will be always your endeavour to get to the highest position and full honour. Your aim is big business, high office, high personality, high class actions, everything of the highest order. Low, small or means, deeds will not be liked by you, nor will you be able to reconcile yourself to such types of work.

It is your powerful and wide a wake personality that has not given way under so much of stress and strain. Any other would have long been finished. Your personality, in the real sense, is flexible. That is why it has withstood so many shocks. You have the experience of both joy and sorrow, hence you are most qualified than others, to give expression to those experiences.

Saturn means service. A person having Saturn prominent in his life is motivated by service. You will therefore serve the people in distress, those who are terrified and worried. Those who are sick will be served by you with pure motive. That service will not have either artificiality or show about it. Whatever you will do in this connection will be motivated by a sense of service. It has become your second nature to keep others happy as far as possible and to serve them. There is no selfishness or show in it, nor is there any intention of self-advertisement through propaganda.

You are not hateful to service. You will not hesitate to do the most menial work or service, if time and circumstances so require it. There must, however, be the basic hint that you would thereby get money. People with

Saturn prominent, will go to any length for money. But the right use of money is known to you much more than is to others. It is to others. It is true, money has value in life and particularly in this material age it is good to earn it and to put in the hardest labour for it. But the value of astrology lies only where it acquaints you with the right path of life. If you are in service, you should realise that your real interest is served, by service in a private firm and there too if it deals with iron or manufacture of iron articles, you have better and early chances for rise. If you are in business you should deal with iron business. To manufature articles of iron, to exchange commodities of iron or to deal with some work which is basically related to iron can lead to your quick rise of luck.

If that is not possible, give next priority to things of black colour. For example you may deal with Tils, Til oil, agency of iron goods. Shani (Saturn) rules over iron and oils. This is a cruel planet. If it is unfavourable it can bring about liquidation. But on the other hand if it is favourable it can make one the master of millions and millions. This root number 8 presides over luck also. Hence you will have more occasions for unexpected gains than others. Being lord of luck, Saturn can give you good luck any moment. It is the nature of Saturn alone that it can turn one into a millionaire in no time and also force him to liquidation in like manner. I would not advise you to enter into speculative business, but would certainly urge you to buy lottery tickets from all the states regularly. While buying the tickets, keep two points in view. Firstly buy the tickets only on the day which is favourable for you. Also try to buy such tickets whose number totals up to the figure 8. Secondly you buy the lottery tickey of a province where lottery is drawn on the dates 8, 17, or 26. If you buy tickets with the above points in your mind, you are sure to be lucky in the favourable transits of planets. It is in your nature that you apply to the task in hand very deligently. At that time you are oblivious even to food and amusement. You do not rest until the task is accomplished.

You have no deep interest in religious maters. Even then, if there is any work connected with some festival, then you put yourself into it heart and soul and leave no stone unturned in making it a success. That is the reason why the managment of societies, sammelans, festivals and parties etc. can entrust the work to you and feel satisfied about the certainty of completion of the work. In fact you ensure that it is satisfactorily completedBut the great hurry and quickness with which you execute the work is not very proper, for later on you repent for the haste. You also suffer due to want of care and neglect. In your keen desire for success you even spend from your own pocket and consequently you have to suffer financially on this account later on. Hence you should undertake such work after due thought and take steps with care to save yourself.

In your life you will have very few moments of amusement for as already stated by me earlier your life is always active and changeful. Hence you sometimes see yourself at the top of success and at other times in the abyss of failure. The greater part of your time is spent in reconciling this contradiction of life leaving very little time to you for amusement. But you will not feel it, for according to you "work is amusement". Thus you will find amusement in a way in the work itself thus enable yourself to act according to the time and circumstance.

You have more than ordinary share of the spirit of dejection for love; loneliness gives rise to being dejected and bored. Besides, introspective people can neither mix up with others easily nor can they talk much. It is also true that people may call you as one with "closed" month yet they would, in your absence praise your actions, honour you and express good thoughts about you.

This is another matter and that is your fear to have unnecessary arguments with any body, to have some accident or to have a quarrel. That would endanger your life and you therefor want to avoid it. IN these days you are very circumspect, somewhat afraid and worried. This is the period when your significator planet saturen is not favourable to you. In such a period it rightly behaves you to be careful and circums pect and not to enter into unnecessary arguments that may harm your career in any way.

You are basically a material minded person who believes in work instead of stone idols as his God. Hence you hate hypocricy and deceit. You will not be able to enter into dhyan by closing eyes and wearing holy white clothes. But at the time of calamity or difficulty you will suddenly be inclined to God.

Then you will spend more time in Pooja and thus you will turn a sort of a believer. But this will be shortlived. You will again return to original path.

As already stated by me you are material minded and as such you consider wealth to the ultimate objective of life. It would be your life's hobby to gather money by this or that means. Whatever the endeavour in life, whatever the lavou its root will be in wealth. The zeal and carefulness wi which you will accumulate wealth would also be applied l you in its non-expenditure. You will be incapable to spe money. Your spending power will be very weak.

Saturn is basically a planet of addiction and vice. Hen if there is slight relaxation of control you will turn towar vice. To have your urge increased towards wine, Bhan opium, Charas or tobacco is not then ruled out. Hence y have to be careful in this regard. It is also clear that on are caught in vice it is very difficult to get rid of it. Lazines inertia, laxity and the like can also hold of you. You a directed by Saturn. Hence your body will be somewhat thi of light dark or wheatish colour, with reddish eyes. Hair w be black and stiff, temperament rather dry and harshness speech all will be very apparent in you. But you should tha Saturn that it has made you wise and experienced from rath early age and has given you the special ability to jud people.

Precautions. It is true that you are clever and practic and capable of influencing others wit your thoughts, still y have some undesirable traits over which it is essential have control.

2. Do not behave untruly with your wife nor try deceive her, for it is very likely that you may be expos and your truth is compromised.

3. Keep control over yourself. Never carry talk fro one quarter to another. This will affect your truth.

4. Try to remove shyness as early as possible. You ha

a tendency to hesitate in meeting any official. You cannot express yourself clearly. You are somewhat afraid. Because of such tendencies you have to cut a sorry figure in interviews.

5. Do not sit tight at any place. On the contrary travel as far as you can, for through travels you are in more profitable situation. As far as possible increase your contacts with the people. Go to their residence. From time to time invite them to your residence. This will make your social field.

6. It is possible your wife may not be keeping good health or she may be a prey to diseases of the nerves or those connected with the stomach. This is not an adequate reason for making your temperament irritable. As far possible you should console her and treat her mentally and psychologically.

7. Don't throw yourself at the mercy of others for your know this results in loss to you. Hence you should actively do work yourself.

8. If you believe that your brothers or your society will help you in any way, this is entirely believed. Neither your brothers nor your relatives can help you. Whatever will happen will be entirely through your own efforts. You are a self-made man. Do not wait for any body to raise you up. Rise yourself.

9. Do not be afraid of enemies. It is possible they may go to the courts of law. It is also possible they may threaten you. All this should not upset you. They cannot touch a hair of yours. You move forward without worry and remain

actively engaged in your work.

10. As far possible, avoid travel to high mountains or swimming in deep waters, for both these situations are not favourable to you. When such situations do arise exercise due care.

11. Do not be entangled in love matters, for this is not your field, your may harm yourself. You cannot profit from women. On the other hand you can lose through them. Hence as far as possible you should get away from this altogether. It is just possible. You may have to swallow the bitter pill of dishonour on this account when planetary situation is weak for you.

12. It is not well to be material minded to the extreme. In life, you should spend more time in worshiping God. They only you can have full solace and satisfaction.

13. Do not allow adamant nature to get control over you. As far as possible try to be tolerent. When you think you can teach others, it is well to remember that sometimes it pays to agree to others' views. Hence always give consideration to the views of others and if necessary act on their advice.

14. Inspite of your great care and wide awareness, you sometimes fall into worry and sorrow. But you are unaware of this and wonder in astonishment how and why there was worry. It is proper for you to take note of your unfavourable time and see that you do not initiate any new business contract or new business transactions in bad time or when the planetary transit is unfavourable.

15. Your temperament is somewhat of a doubting nature. You should not give much room to doubt. To doubt or distrust your wife is not proper.

16. It is true, money has importance in life and is the prop of this age. But you should not turn to any low act for the sake of money. You should not do any act that should distort your personality or create difficulty for it.

17. Do not be sad for your future. Nor it is proper for you to cry over fate. Whatever happens, let it happen. Everything will be alright by themselves. In the dark terrain of future, there is bound to come some ray of light. You should mind only one thing viz, your concern is only with duty and not with the fruits thereof. Fruits should be left to God or to Nature.

18. Loneliness and restrictiveness are not proper in life. You will slowly by bored and feel isolated. Hence sit with your friends and well wishers. Give them your time and attention.

19. It is possible your life might have been full of thorns. This does not mean in future that you will meet with thorns only. The future is definitely strewn with flowers. The only need for you is to get forward and select the right path.

20. You should not remain inactive. Even otherwise it is not possible for you to sit idle. When you will become thus dejected, you will revolt against yourself and throw away the work in hand. But this is not proper. The control of yourself is your speciality.

21. Keep your self free from unneceessary worries.

Everyone will see to his own problem. How far can you solve the problem of others? Hence as far as possible restrict yourself.

22. The way you are making progress is alright. Do not try to take too long a jump, for by so doing, you would neither reach the others share not regain the lost ground.

23. Do not entangle yourself in the love of any women for saying your own wife. This brings not only loss of wealth but is in vain. Hence to waste time is not wise.

24. Be away from intoxicants as far as possible, for it you are once in the grip of an intoxicant you will not be able to easily get out of it. And this will, in a way be a sign of your fall.

25. Instead of being irritated, disturbed or upset try to feel yourself light. Give room to smiles and happiness. Then only is life meaningful.

Health: It has been stated above that your planet is mainly airy in nature. Hence you will be afflicted off and on b heart troubles. You will also suffer from constipation and inteatinal troubles etc.

2. In old age you will have diseases like gout, blood-pressure, heart-trouble, anemia, blood pollutions, headache and weakness of limbs. Hence you have to exercise preventive care in time.

3. You should give attention to vitamins A, D and E, for due to shortage of these you may suffer off and on. Hence consult your doctor from time to time.

4. You can suffer at any time from any of the diseases like leprosy, breathing trouble, blood pollution, fever, baldness, weakness of the urinary bladder, passing of urine with burning sensation, pain in nose and ears, bleeding etc. Hence to be careful of these ailments is very proper and necessary for you.

5. You should make use of green vegetables as far as possible. Vegetables like spinach, mintch, corriander leaves, Bethua raw or boiled are very useful for you. Hence make maximum use of these.

6. The use of fruits is also very useful and necessary for you.

Weak Time: People having 8 as their root number should always keep in view their weak time. For your planet Saturn is subject to quiet changes of goodness and badness. It can make one a millionaire and with a little neglect throw one in the ditch of fall. December, January, March and April are unfavourable months for you. Besides when Saturn is weak, retrograde or eclipsed time is also not favourable for you. Hence in this period take care of your health. Also so not initiate any big transaction or new item of business.

Strong Time: You should always be alert towards your strong time. For your strong time is excellent which can give you benefit of lakhs. From this point of view the period between 20th September to 25th October and 20th January to 20th February can be said to be strong and most favourable for you.

Good Dates: Your root number is 8. Hence, 8, 17 and 26th of every month can be said to be the most favourable dates for you. If you combine good dates with strong time and then initiate your important undertakings, you can remain in a profitable situation from every point of view.

Good Days: Saturday is the best day for you. Any work, if initiated on Saturdays, will prove good and favourable.

Good Colour: Black, blue, gray and purple are lucky colours for you. If possible, you must keep a ker-chief of black colour in your pocket. This will keep obstacles and worries away from you.

Good gems: Your lucky gem is Saphire Turquise- "Neelam". It is called Neelamani in Sanskrit. Neelvil yakut in Persian. It has 5 prominent qualities.

1. It has blue colour
2. It is shining and seems to be emanating rays from it.
3. It is smooth.
4. It is transparent.
5. It has symmetrical corners.

Get a ring of Pancha Dhatu and get embedded in it Neelam of 5 Ratties weight and then wear it on the middle finger. This undoubtedly removes all obstacles.

Friendship: All men and women who have 8 as their root number of whose date of birth is 8, 17 or 26 can prove good friends to you. Besides, if you examine you will find people born on 2, 4, 8, 12, 16, 20, 24, 26 dates also helpful and favourable. Hence at times of engaging a servant, entering into a business or partnership, you keep these numbers of people in view and you will surely gain a profitable situation.

Good Years: Your root number is 8, hence 8, 17, 26, 35, 44, 53, 62, 71, 80, 89 years of your life will be favourable and promotors of well-being. Besides the years that have been stated to be good for people having root numbers 2 and 4 are also favourable for you. Again, those years which are divisible by 8 will also prove important. For example in future the years 1976, 1984, 1992, 2000, 2008, 2016, 2024 and 2032 will also be lucky and weal promoting.

You are really brave and can face calamities with confidence, like a lamp that continues to burn even in cyclone. You will rise high that is certain.

Notable Personalities: Prominent and noteworthy persons who have 8 as their root number:

S. No.	Names	Born on	Root No.
1.	Queen Mary	26 May	8
2.	Joseph Chamberiain	8 July	8
3.	GeorgeBernard Shaw	25 July	8
4.	Prince Albert	26 August	8
5.	Amiral Dewey	26 December	8
6.	Sir Humphry Davy	17 December	8
7.	J.D. Rockfeller	8 July	8
8.	Dr. Zakir Hussain	8February	8
9.	Guru Nanak Dev	8 November	8

10.	Harry S. Truman	8 May	8
11.	Haider Ali	8 December	8
12.	C. Rajagopalachari	8 December	8
13.	Mao Tse Tung	26 December	8

Root No: 9

English dates : 9, 18 and 27.

The number 9 is most shining, fiercely burning, full of light and with fierce rays. Its representative planet is Mars who shines most in the sky like a burning coal. By nature full of anger, strong of resolve, prepared to die for honour, such a planet has its own distinctive importance, which separates it from others.

Mars presides as deity over wars and always believes to kill and be killed. It cannot brook defeat or insult. It does not want to spend life emitting slow smoke from a piece of wood. It wants to live like gunpowder ready to blow and shine. It believes in living for a short period but living with dignity and thereby surprise the world.

Mars is a very powerful planet. Hence people with 9 as their root number do not deem it fit to live under somebody. They do not believe in living begging, but in independent conscious living. They believe in surprising the world with their deeds.

People with 9 as their root number are during, both physically and mentally. But sometimes their daring goes to extremes and becomes adamancy and sometimes this devil-daring results in tragedy. But this does not deter them or frighten them. They have immeasurable push, firm resolve and bravery.

These are such brave people who exhibit wonderful and astonishing deeds and hoist their flag of everlasting fame. To have the weight of an elephant over their chests, to pass through the valleys of death in search of inaccessible mountain peaks, to explore the snowbound regions of the northern and southern poles, to jump into fire, to go hunting into dreadful territories of South Africa and thereby earn fame, are such acts of extreme daring which can be cited as examples. Such examples are set by such people with number 9. Even though such people appear from exterior surface to be aggressive and explosive but are soft like rose from inside. Apparently they are hard and disciplinarians but at heart they are compassionate and full of human milk. Hence while they are capable of establishing standards of discipline, they are also popular with their subordinates. They take the responsibility of making the most adamant of persons yield and fulfill that responsibility. And at occasions, they are so drowned in their false prestige that they fail to see their own wellbeing. Such people will like to live with pomp and show to show their prowess, but the reality would be the other way round. Such people believe in maximum of window-dressing. When the position of the planet Mars in the heavens is favourable, these people achieve success in their mission and undertakings and walk with added speed towards their goal, which they attain whatever its nature. But when Mars is weak they have to see so many ups and down that they break down inside.

Precautions: It is necessary for you to remain wide awake, alert and soft. When the planetary position in the heavens is weak, the following events can take place in your life sometimes.

1. At the time of weak planetary situation, the temperament of fight will take the upper hand in you. The brain will be caught in a strange affiction and you will develop hot temper. Who knows you may explode on a little talk and by whom. Nothing can be predicted it.

2. Though you would try to remain calm but this is not in your hands. A situation which you ignore at the time of strong position of planets will be the one on which will readily entangle yourself.

3. Even ordinarily you do not give much importance to the officials, but in these days you will not count them more than mere straws. Whatever work, they may entrust to you, you will use lethargy, neutrality and coldness to it. When questioned, you will give irrelevant answers. You will fell yourself that it does happen like that and that till sometime back you were alright; what has happened in the interval.

4. Your rift with your wife will continue. You cannot reconcile your view's with hers. This is true, but in these days you will be off your balance at every step and chide her and sometimes you will go to the length of defaming her in public. There seems to be very little possiblity of having a wholesome married life.

5. In such days your wife will fall sick and she will suffer from blood pollution, falling away of hair, weakness, hysteria, epilepsy, stoppage of menses, or bleeding and the

like, as a result of which you will have to devote much of your time to her in addition to spending much or her leading to the unblanching of your budget.

6. In these days you may be involved in law suits too. Someone will falsely implicate you in a law suit or will insult you for which you may have to knock at the door of law regularly. This vicious resort to law courts will continue in life. Ligigation is also possible in these days on days on account of landed property or the houses.

7. If you are employed at a place, which has electric power or is related to explosive articles, you have to be all the more careful. In the event of your service being connected with the electric wires, you should, as far as possible, protect your hands and feet.

8. If your are a hunter you should postpone hunting for sometime, for the time is against you If you have to go hunting don't take too much risk in any case. Always be careful and alert.

9. You will fall sick in these days and will suffer through diseases relating to blood. You will get rid of one disease while another will crop up.

10. In these days you will have more occasions for accidents. These accidents may be physical, emotional or social. Death of parents, separation from wife, separation from your son, accident through car, motor cycle or scooter, to turn mad, any of these tragedies are possible in these days. Hence as far as possible be alert and have full control over your senses.

11. As stated above you are brave and daring and believe in challenging the adversary and giving him a crushing defeat but during the period of weak planetary position you will attack stealthily or will try take undue advantage of the weakness of the adversary. But soon after you will curse yourself for such a cowardly behaviour. Your family tradition has not been of such low type and hence you should not do any such unbecoming act.

12. In old age you feel more, weak and will slowly fall prey to impotency. You should, therefore, control your body and character in youth itself.

13. It is possible for many women to enter your life. You cannot escape it. You will not realize its ill effects during your youth but in old age you will fell worried and will be full of regrets.

14. Wine and other intoxicant will be started by you in youth. In the beginning this vice will be contacted through friends and thereafter its use will increase for the purpose of drawing away sorrow. Situation may arise when you may cross all limits of drinking. You should, therefore, control it from the very beginning. Arise: seek means to escape it, for in old age these situations can prove very harmful to you.

15. There will be disease connected with the blood or heart in one shape or the other. You cannot get rid of them completely. In rip old age you have troubles like pressure too.

16. Try to get rid of false pride, show and window-dressing as soon as possible. For you yourself believe that these are mere hypocricy and are of no advantage. How long

can you therefore, afford to be showy.

17. Hurry is the greatest weakness or your character. If someone speaks you to give your verdict, you give the same, even before fully hearing him. You are after finishing every work in haste, even if it may harm you. Must have felt often that had you not acted with hurry you could have done a work more efficiently. Due to this habit of hurry you are many a time prey to misunderstanding. Hence you should neither do any act in hurry nor establish deep relations with anybody without due thought. Then alone there will be meaning in your life.

18. It is not proper for your personality to show your enthusiasm or get angry at trifles. Solve all the problems and situations with coolness. Aggressiveness and violence are traits or animals, not yours.

19. Don't enter into litigation. So far as possible solve the matter by mutual discussion. Litigation through courts can only lead you to difficulties and you will thereby only add to your problems. Your life is meant for the completion of some more important work. To spend time and money on these small things does not become you.

20. It is the misfortune of number 9 people that they get enemies without desiring them. People with whom there was friendship or intimacy till yesterday are today bent upon destroying you root and branch. Increase the number of your friends. You root and branch. Increase the number of your friends. Your cleverness lies in removing the differences from the minds of your enemies and trying to make them agreeable to you.

21. Do not sign on any paper in haste, even though it may appear to contain conditions set forth by yourself. You should so contrive that you get a day or two consider it. When you are satisfied alround, then only you should dign it.

22. Never keep any explosive articles in your house. Do not have in your house, inflammable articles, petrol, crackers, poison etc. In fact you must have experienced it that when you are in rage you are prepared to do the worst and in such mental unpreparedness it will not be a matter of surprise, if you even commit suicide.

23. You will have enemies but the number of your friends will also be not inconsiderable. These friends will always be prepared to help you in every way. After the age of 30 you will have a friend who will not mince matters and tell you everything on face and will prove to you a very infinite and a true guide. He would not only save you from all dangers in life but will also help you in making your life prosperous.

24. As far as possible, save yourself from a situation leading to operation whether of yourself, or your wife or of your child, for operation is not favourable to you. Once you make a strong resolve not to go in for operation, you will see that your problem has been solved even without an operation and the disease etc. for which operation was originally considered necessary has been removed.

25. As already stated above you are a self-respecting person; one ready to lay down life for the sake or honour. As a result you are enraged at every unfavourable situation

and when enraged your only aim is to finish your adversary completely. I would advise you to save yourself from this emotionalism. Such high rage, such great feelings of revenge, such high irritability of temper does not become you. You should adapt yourself to the time and circumstances.

26. As far as possible you should settle your own problems. You need not involve yourself with the problems of others. Nor should you arrange for the panchayat for solving problems for others; for it is neither in your interest nor proper.

27. You should arrange to create an order out of disorder that exists in your family. You can see that it is because of you that there is an atmosphere of dreadfulness. Peace is nowhere to be seen in the house. You should have poise and pay attention towards creating an atmosphere of activity and happiness in the house.

28. Whenever it is a question of property transaction, rest assured, you will get by it. You will profit whether the transaction relates to the purchase or sale of property or its commission. You can earn from this type of work and as such you should not try to suffer a loss through your haste and hurry. You will see it for yourself that no sooner the planetary position is favourable to you; you stand to profit by such business.

29. Let smile spread itself on your face. To have a strict appearance on the face may be good for discipline but it can throw you miles apart for social life and can reduce your popularity. Hence try to keep yourself happy and attractive.

It can be tested in two ways:

(1) If you put it in milk you will observe a sort of reddish shadow. (2) If it is placed on a piece of paper or cotton in sunshine these articles catch fire.

At auspicious time, get coral weighing 5 Ratties embeded in a golden ring in such a way that it touches your skin when the ring is worn. Such a ring worn will prove instrumental in removing all obstacles and take you to the path of progress and prosperity.

Friendship: You should select your friends with utmost care, for it is generally your friends who have acted against you and deceived you. Men and women with their date of birth as 9, 18, or 27 can prove trustworthy and helpful to you. While selecting a wife also, bear the same thing in mind. You should also know that people born with root number 9 and at a time which is " Strong" for you, will surely prove fully helpful to you. It will also be beneficial for you to keep the above dates in view while engaging a new servant, having a new partner, etc.

Good years: Since number 9 is very important in your life the years 9, 18, 27, 36, 45, 54, 63, 72, 81 and 90 in life will prove favourable, weal promoting, eventful and tending to progress. Besides, the years that are divisible by 9 will also be favourable be tending to progress 1971, 1980, 1989 and 1998 etc.

In fact you are lucky in more than one sense by being a person with root number 9. You are brave and powerful, you can give a tough fight in the practical field of life. Hence arise and perform such deeds as should make the world wonder and shower praise on you.

Notable personalities: Prominent and noteworthy personalities of the world with 9 as their root number:

S. No.	Name	Born on	Root No.
1.	King Edward	9 November	9
2.	Theodore Roosevelt	27 October	9
3.	Lord Curzon	9 February	9
4.	Earnest Renau	27 February	9
5.	Elizabeth (Australia)	18 August	9
6.	Nicholas	18 May	9
7.	George Stephenson	9 May	9
8.	Omar Khayyam	18 May	9
9.	Onasis	9 September	9
10.	Doris Duke	18 December	9
11.	President Johnson	27 August	9
12.	Om Prakash Sharma (Publisher)	27 November	9
13.	Shri Chaitanya Mahaprabhu	18 February	9
14.	John Milton	9 December	9
15.	Rama Krishna Paramhansa	18 February	9
16.	Shri Golwalker	18 February	9